Advance Praise for *The 100 Thing Challenge*

"Reading Dave Bruno's book has been both bracing (to think what could be done!), but also a challenge (should I get rid of some or all those books?). Living simply is only an ideal until someone like Bruno gets particular. The way he got particular should make everyone think—hard, which is a very good thing."

—Mark Noll, Francis A. McAnaney Professor of History,
University of Notre Dame

"In a loving, wise, sometimes hilarious manner, Dave Bruno holds a mirror up to us and says to take a closer look at how we're living. He's no Don Quixote, tilting at imaginary windmills. His concerns and solutions are real and realistic. Reading this will lead you to a better life."

—Dean Nelson, author of *God Hides in Plain Sight* and director of
the journalism program at Point Loma Nazarene University

About the Author

DAVE BRUNO is an author and advocate for simple living. He's the creator of the 100 Thing Challenge, a project focused on breaking free from the constraints of American-style consumerism. Bruno loves every outdoor square inch of California that he's ever hiked, biked, surfed, or visited. He lives in San Diego with his wife and three daughters. Bruno's favorite of many household pets is his loyal mutt, Piper.

HARPER

NEW YORK • LONDON • TORONTO • SYDNEY

The

100 Thing

Challenge

How I Got Rid of Almost Everything,
Remade My Life, and Regained My Soul

Dave Bruno

HARPER

HarperCollins books may be purchased for educational, business, or sales promotional use. For information please write: Special Markets Department, HarperCollins Publishers, 10 East 53rd Street, New York, NY 10022.

FIRST EDITION

Designed by Sunil Manchikanti

Library of Congress Cataloging-in-Publication Data is available upon request.

ISBN 978-0-06-178774-4

11 12 13 14 15 ID/RRD 10 9 8 7 6 5 4 3 2 1

To my friends and to the friends I have made:

That we may live joyful and thoughtful lives

on earth, not remembered for our

possessions. Instead, let us be known

for the gifts that come from our hearts.

For he will not much remember the days of his

life because God keeps him occupied with joy in

his heart.

ECCLESIASTES 5:20

Contents

Preface

Of Cats and Contentment

A t thirty-eight years old, I can say that in many ways I have realized the good life, or at least a plausible version of it. I am writing this book in my relatively large house comfortably situated at the end of a cul-de-sac. It is located in an award-winning master-planned suburban development in Southern California. Most evenings I can stand on the deck above our garage and watch the sun sink over the Pacific Ocean about ten miles away.

I have a beautiful wife who is a talented cook, parents marvelously, and loves to read and discuss thoughtful books. Together we have helped God create three daughters, all of whom are healthy and have excelled in their various activities. We are free of credit card debt. My career, first in technology, then as an entrepreneur in the publishing industry, and now in marketing at a university, has helped fund my contented middle-class lifestyle. Also, very generous parents have pitched in along the way.

I also own a dog. Piper is lying at my feet right now as I write. He is a mutt we rescued from the shelter. We think he is a cross between a German shepherd and a Rhodesian ridgeback. He is fast as lightning, has a keen nose, and is faithful to me.

Then there is the cat we have living with us. If anywhere, that is the place my good life starts to break down. Though I have a measure of affection for our cat, domesticated felines have their own agenda. Perhaps that is why no one talks about cats and the good life. For example, have you ever heard anyone mention a cat and the American dream in the same sentence? We tend to believe that opportunity has an agenda set by those of us who pursue it. Cats disagree. Unlike dogs, cats are absorbed by their personal concerns, not the aspirations of their owners.

But our house backs up to a field of coastal sage shrub that is home to a pack of coyotes. Those coyotes have been dining on neighborhood cats for years. Last spring they finally ate Eustace Clarence Scrubb, one of ours. Scrubb was a feral cat we adopted after he fell off the roof of our friend's parents' house and lost track of his cat family. Two weeks after Scrubb was eaten we replaced him with a new cat from the shelter we called Crisp. Our other cat, Beatrice, was indignant at the speed with which we exchanged Scrubb. She sulked for months, and I know why. She had finally learned a hard truth. Even cats must submit to human notions of the good life, in that cats can be substituted with remarkable nonchalance.

We talk about the good life or the American dream as if it were permanent, as if it were the finish line of a race. We say that we have "arrived at the American dream." We announce that we are "living the good life." And yet it has been my experience that, at least in our times, the good life and the American dream are more obsolescent than obtainable. A pet cat is never fully content, but let's be honest, whether you're a cat lover or not, domesticated kitties are replaceable. So, too, is everything we feel we need in order to be satisfied with our lives. We buy things year after year, over and over again, in our pursuit of contentment. It has been my impression that these days, replacement is emblematic of our dreams more than ownership. This is a curiosity, for it is by endlessly acquiring the right things that we measure our distance from the good life. We are always getting, but never getting there.

That was my observation as well as my personal experience. For much of my life I endeavored not for objects I could settle down with and enjoy, but just for new stuff. Too often this was my achievement: not working hard to earn some special thing, but rather, after tucking that special something away, going back out to the mall to buy again.

The 100 Thing Challenge, which my book describes, was one of several responses to the unsettled feeling I developed after years of living a life filled with stuff instead of contentment—after arriving at a reasonable version of the American dream and still groping for more. I felt I might be chasing after what was not mine to have, and what I could never get anyway. It occurred to me that I felt less like myself and more like someone I should not be.

I was about to change that feeling.

Part One

The Challenge
Takes Shape

1. The 100 Thing Challenge

ere in Southern California we San Diegans have a saying. Hawaiians wouldn't appreciate it, but we say it nonetheless. We go outside, look around, and then say, "Just another day in paradise."

The saying fits most every day of the year. In San Diego, near the ocean, it's never bitterly cold and it's never oppressively hot. I can appreciate the realities of the nonsublime weather in certain areas of the country. I spent a few years in Chicago for college, before heading back to San Diego. Then I returned to the Chicago area for two years of graduate school. I have figured that in the five years (sixty months) that I spent in the Midwest, forty months consisted of glacial winter. Another seventeen months were hot, airless summer. Perhaps three months over the entire five years were pleasant. Maybe even a day or two could have been described as idyllic. San Diego is different from that. Every five years we have about sixty months of heavenly weather.

On a July day a few years back, the weather was at its finest. The sun was shining about seventy-eight degrees warm. A cool offshore ocean breeze was wafting through the open windows of our house. If ever I might have been justified in exclaiming, "Just another day in paradise," this was the day. But I didn't. I couldn't muster the words. I was agitated. In fact, I got so worked up that I had a crisis. A small, domestic crisis but a crisis nonetheless. The episode precipitated an epiphany or a eureka moment, or both. And in that short time, I found myself grumbling, "I am taking the 100 Thing Challenge."

Even accounting for my eccentricities, that is a pretty unusual thing for me to say, so let me backtrack and explain what happened. On that Saturday, I was juggling a fairly industrious middle-class American lifestyle. My family consisted of my wife, Leanne, and my young daughters, Lucy, Phoebe, and Bridget, who all demanded my attention, which, I should say, I have always been happy to give them. Well, usually. Also I liked to hike in the mountains and desert. (In addition to perfect weather and proximity to the ocean, San Diego is close to mountains and deserts.) The dog needed walking closer to home and the cats needed to be kept safe from hungry coyotes. I owned a guitar that I would play every other night. I had my aspirational hobby, woodworking, which I turned my attention to once a weekend. I made a living with my day job in the marketing department of nearby Point Loma Nazarene University. On the side, I ran an audiobook publishing business, ChristianAudio. And I had been blogging for a few years, mostly railing against excessive consumerism, at StuckInStuff.com. Basically, I was a husband and father; an outdoorsy, animal-loving, wannabe singer-songwriter; an entrepreneur; a likes-to-use-his-hands kind of guy who also felt a compulsion to write. And because I did all of these things, I had my own desk. It sat near my bed for the sake of convenience. It sometimes got messy.

On this weekend day in July 2007, our family had spent quite a bit of time cleaning up the house. We picked up and trimmed the yard. We vacuumed the carpet and swept the bamboo floors downstairs. We did laundry and hung clothes. We crammed toys into closets and onto shelves. Eventually, I turned my attention to my business and made my way to the home office desk to look for something I was working on at the time. After one glance at the desk, I knew there wasn't a chance on God's green earth that I was going to find it. Things had gotten out of control. Objects on my desk were absorbed into an undifferentiated mass of clutter.

When I surveyed the hopelessness of the situation, I did what any emotionally healthy person would do: I procrastinated. I put off my entrepreneurial piece of business, and instead I wandered into my bedroom closet a dozen feet away. But when I walked from the mess of the home office desk and into the closet, the mess hadn't left me.

The closet in our bedroom is a walk-in type with plenty of room for clothes, shoes, belts, hats, odds and ends, and even the empty luggage that we keep on the upper shelves. I keep one corner for storing my adventure gear. A backpack and tent fit in that corner, and my sleeping bag hangs from a nail near the ceiling. There was room for almost anything I might want to fit into that closet, except me. I stood there, not easily able to move, and I started to panic a little.

We had just cleaned up the house. A lot. And I should let you know, we're not particularly materialistic people who intentionally collect an abundance of things. We don't live by the rule "The person who dies with the most toys wins." In fact, we have tried to live by that rule's antithesis. Over the years we've given many things away to people who need stuff more than us. We've tried to resist constant consumer acquisition. Our family has not lived like a family of hermits, we've just tried to live simply. But after we had spent the weekend cleaning and tidying, my desk and my closet didn't seem to belong to a person who claimed to live a thrifty life.

I left the upstairs and went down to the kitchen for a drink of ice water. The kitchen in our house is long and rectangular and it has counter space with twelve drawers. Four of them are junk drawers. A full thirty-three percent of the sliding storage space in our kitchen is devoted to knickknacks, things we rarely if ever use and that we couldn't make a penny on if we tried to unload them at a garage sale. Things like keys for locks we no longer have, broken flashlights and their spent batteries, and a first-generation blue iPod Mini that no longer turns on. When I counted the junk drawers, I did not include the two drawers so stuffed full of kitchen utensils that we have trouble closing them and sometimes cannot even open them. And I didn't count the two drawers bursting with dishcloths. I hesitate to mention the fifteen cabinets. Let's just say that there were enough pots, pans, cookbooks, coffee fixings, vases, toys, craft supplies, and Tupperware crammed into them to guarantee that something would fall out every time one of them was opened. And there's no way I'm going to discuss the pantry. All this wasn't news to me, but I was looking at the situation differently. My panic began to mature into worry.

Our kitchen has a door that opens to the garage. Back then, when I went through that door I could take only one step before having to stop and make a hard left-hand turn. The turn was necessary because one pace into the garage, things started to pile up. Situated one stride in front of the door there was an old collapsible bookshelf we had bought at Target. I had jury-rigged it to store long-armed woodworking clamps. The shelves also held a random-orbit sander, an eighteen-volt cordless circular saw, two drills, dozens of bits, a three-decades-old Sears Craftsman router, two antique hand planes, a hardly used socket wrench set, a remote-controlled model of a Mini Cooper, a flashlight (always worthlessly low on battery power), and a never-used laser level from QVC, which my mom had bought for me and for each of the men of the family one Christmas.

Our two-car garage had room for, oh, just a few other things. There were two workbenches. (I'm on a roll here complaining, but let me pause and let you know that I made one of those workbenches with three glued-up sheets of hardwood ply, poplar trim, and an antique vise I found on eBay. It was *so* sweet.) There was also a router table and a new router, an Australian-made Triton 2¼-horsepower plunge router, one of the best routers in the world. And resting against the wall near the router table was a sheet of particle board with a large piece of glass attached to it; this I used as a sharpening station for hand plane blades. That is done by securing various grit sandpapers to the ultraflat surface of the glass and using them to little by little hone the blades.

The workbenches and router table were not unlike the home office desk. It wasn't easy to find all the things I had on them, like nails, screws, hammers, screwdrivers, files, wrenches, awls, twine, insecticides, lubricant, glue, and craft putty. Did I mention I was trying to build a model train layout? I needed to do something with the three boxes, each containing hundreds of pieces, of German Märklin toy trains and track that I had collected over the years.

Oh, and then there was the rock climbing wall that stretched across the back of the garage. And the floor-to-ceiling shelving I had built along the length of the far wall to store the sixteen storage containers full of Christmas, Valentine's Day, Easter, Fourth of July, and Halloween decorations, and also the family camping gear. (Recall that my personal camping gear was stored in my closet, since I am more fastidious about caring for adventure gear than the other adult in our family.) Above the garage door were the hanging shelves I had built to store eight more containers full of old files, rundown battery-powered toys, and extra American Girl dolls, who took turns sleeping for months in clear plastic tubs while their peers competed for loving attention with dozens of other toys in the house.

...

Walking around our house and garage that day, I physically tripped on nothing. But inside, I ran into some hard stuff. I realized I was a hypocrite. *Ouch!* I was griping on my blog about how consumerism is ruining people's lives, even as all of my possessions, and the things I helped my wife and daughters collect, were overrunning our home.

I had to admit that I had a problem. *Ugh!* I was telling people to shun consumerism even as I continued to participate in it myself. It dawned on me: I was aware of the problem of consumerism. I had come up with the perfect name for it and used it for my blog's title, Stuck In Stuff. I was able to articulate the hindrance of consumerism. But I had not found and taken the actions that would free me from its constraints.

In fact, over the years, one way I had escaped the paralysis of feeling stuck in stuff was to get away from the mess by going to the store to look for more things. My path to the store was paved with good intentions, like going to find a solution for storing all our stuff in a neat and orderly way. But I couldn't help myself. More than a few times I had taken a break from spring cleaning to browse storage containers at Target, only to come home with a new flashlight or set of colored pencils or picture frame that I found on one of the store's evil bargain end caps. Or I had stared at a pile of shoes on the floor of my closet, each made for its different function, and thought, "Why?" And then I would find myself at REI looking for a pair of crossover shoes that could serve multiple purposes, like hiking and casual wear. That is how, again with good intentions, I often turned two pairs of shoes into three.

But most troubling of all, on that summer day I saw that I was living my scariest nightmare. My desire to live a meaning-ful life was getting forestalled by the petty, day-to-day demands of all my stuff.

As I stood in my garage, I realized that it was not just that all the stuff created a mess, requiring valuable time to clean up. That was true, but that wasn't the worst of it. I realized it was not the clutter, the overaccumulation of things, but rather the *things themselves* that were taking my attention away from what mattered in my life. Camping gear was getting my atten-tion, not being outside. Tools were taking up my time, not using them to be creative. Toys were distracting me from the fun of playing. My things were not doing what they were meant to do: serve a greater purpose than possession alone.

In that moment I came to see that I had not merely mis-placed a piece of paper on my desk. At some point in my life before I lost the paper, I had lost my freedom. Of all people on earth, I thought there was no way it could happen to me. But I was a slave to my belongings. Maybe all my possessions were having fun bossing me around, yet I felt miserable.

I returned to the house contemplative. I climbed the stairs and went to look in the mirror located in our bedroom. That's a place I have stood before. Whenever it is time to make a hard decision in my life, I go there. In the past, I had stood in front of the mirror and looked myself in the eye and inquired about my career. I had asked if I wanted to see myself five years later working at the same go-nowhere job that wasn't doing anything of value for the world. I had answered no.

Back then I responded to that negative answer with the positive energy it took to become an entrepreneur. I started an audiobook company that prioritized publishing the many thoughtful religious titles that had been passed over by other audiobook publishers. I even came up with the company's tag line, "Listen Enjoy Think Grow," because I believe that joyfulness and thoughtfulness are both necessary components of spiritual maturity. If I was going to be responsible for starting a company, I wanted it to be an organization that helped people be better humans. For the years that I was running ChristianAudio with my business partners, I was able to look in the mirror and see a person I felt was doing something of value for the world. But lately that feeling of doing good work had shrunk away. I'd done something to change my impression of myself from a professional standpoint but I didn't feel quite whole.

Now, as I stood there looking, I recognized something was missing. I was a person living a half-truth. I believed that material possessions would overwhelm my life and keep me from meaningful pursuits unless I did something about it, but I had not actually done much by way of a response. I was looking at a person with ideas but without much action. It wasn't a pleasant sight. And yet, rather than seeing only despair, I caught a little twinkle in my eye. I was galvanized to action. I wrote about it on my blog that weekend: "I have an idea. A spontaneous idea that might change my life forever. I'm calling it the 100 Thing Challenge. And I'm taking it."

Oh yeah, my life changed all right.

2. A Reluctant Entrepreneur

The 100 Thing Challenge developed after I had been running my own business for four years. But in the few months before the challenge occurred to me, I had started reassessing my role in the workplace as a business owner, as an entrepreneur. At around the same time, in the same month, in fact, I decided to fundamentally alter my relationship to the world as a consumer and also made the first move toward selling my share of the business. Each was an impulse toward a simpler, less stressful, and more contemplative life, perhaps, but each move also represented a reaction against something. What I found in that time is that the entrepreneur's drive is not unlike the impulse that confronts us at the mall, the ill effects of what I call American-style consumerism. It is the compulsion for more and more. There is no stasis at the mall, unless it is to catch your breath on a bench in order to rest up for more shopping. And as I ran a business, I came to realize that the natural inclination of the entrepreneur, which has been reinforced by our business culture, is the same as that of the shopper.

Initially this entrepreneurial drive is a good and necessary bent. Without it, all but the luckiest small businesses would fail, because it is exceedingly difficult to start a company. Without the resilience to keep trying to get bigger despite adversity, small businesses wouldn't overcome the trials of starting up. Not only that, it is an obvious requirement that a new company grow. But how much? Anyone experienced in business knows that too much growth too quickly is as fatal as no growth at all. But when is it fine to slow down, or even stop? Most experienced business owners would say that there's never a time to slow down or stop growing. (The exception, of course, is an economic recession that forces slow growth or stagnation. Who considers that a good business circumstance?)

There is a similar necessity for the adult consumer. Perhaps some people who strike out from their childhood house on their own overdo it when purchasing the things they need to establish a home of their own. But they do need to get some stuff. What I found in my own life, and what helped push me over the top to do the 100 Thing Challenge, was that the purchasing never stopped. From the time when Leanne and I began to establish a home of our own, I was always buying more and more stuff. It was as if setting up a new home never ended. As if the very notion of "setting up" implied endlessly recurring activity and never resting. When is it fine to slow down the buying or even stop shopping altogether? Most marketers and consumers alike would say that there's never a time to slow down acquiring stuff, let alone to stop entirely. (In my consumer experience, the exceptions were the times when we could not pay for or didn't have—or couldn't stomach—the credit to charge the things we wanted. Who considers not having enough money to buy all the things they want a good consumer circumstance?)

That same feeling of repetitiveness was known to me as a consumer and it was known to me as an entrepreneur. The desire *itself,* to get more and to grow more, increased. There was no end in sight.

I remember chatting with a fellow entrepreneur once. He had sold a couple of businesses, was running another, and in his spare time worked in the ministry starting new churches. I reflected on how I had my hands in a few different business opportunities. There was another opportunity on the near horizon. "Someday," I mused, "I hope to have just one thing going with a lot of free time on my hands."

"No you don't," he shot back, too sure of himself and me for my liking. "I've made peace with it. We entrepreneurs can never rest."

The expectation of the consumer in American-style consumerism is to buy and buy and buy some more. The expected route for a small business in American-style capitalism is to grow and grow and grow some more. The anticipation is the same, as well. Both the shopper and the entrepreneur behave as if there is an end goal of contentment. But neither ever quits striving for that satisfaction. There's always a little more stuff to be had. There's always a little more profit to be had.

I was prompted to rethink my consumption goals at the same time that I reconsidered the aims of my vocation as an entrepreneur. I liked Bill McKibben's ideas about creating businesses and communities focused on "durability" instead of growth. In his book *Deep Economy,* he says that such businesses and communities "may well yield less stuff, but they produce richer relationships; they may grow less quickly, if at all, but they make up for it in durability."* Durable things last. That is more than most people these days can say about their stuff or their jobs.

. . .

My entrepreneurial disposition manifested itself early in my life. I repeated first grade because of my restless energy and my natural inclination to resist established power structures. Later, I wandered through a community college, a state university, a Bible institute, and eventually graduate school at a liberal arts college. My, let's call it "varied," education in the humanities in no way pointed toward the career I eventually found myself in, technology. But wandering about institutions where I never felt settled did foreshadow my urge to start my own thing outside of a preexisting company.

I actually became an entrepreneur on a Monday morning in 2004 at a Starbucks. My buddy Cory and I had been meeting once a week for about a year to chat about life and gripe about our day jobs. On that morning he proposed that we start a business. (How many businesses have been dreamed up in a Starbucks? A number, I warrant. Maybe more good ideas than have come to people spontaneously in their garages; maybe not.) I was working for my father's technology consulting company without hope for purposeful work or future career development, and Cory was also suffering the daily grind. Cory had a longer commute than me, so he listened to audiobooks. After a year of commuting hours each day, he ran out of books he wanted to listen to. He discovered many of the best-selling Christian titles that he enjoyed reading had not been made into audiobooks.

* Bill McKibben, *Deep Economy: The Wealth of Communities and the Durable Future* (New York: Times Books, 2007), 2.

His idea was to start a publishing company to fill that gap in the market. I liked it.

Two days later, on Wednesday morning, I marched to my employer and asked to go part-time. This wasn't an easy conversation, but it wasn't too difficult since it was a talk with my dad, who, though I'm sure it stung him to know I didn't want to stick around his company forever, is kind and has always been supportive of my plans. Plus the reality was that things were pretty slow in San Diego, and most of my dad's technology consulting clients were in the San Francisco Bay area. My part-time status wasn't really going to affect his company.

Two days after the conversation with my dad, on Friday morning, Cory and I met again at the same Starbucks. Being a little dramatic for effect, I announced to him that I had quit my "full-time" job. We started a company on that day.

We first drafted our business plan on a Starbucks napkin. (We should have saved and framed it.) Within a week, though, I had bought a special journal and pencil to use for the task of scribbling down strategies and action items. We had crazy ideas of what we thought we needed to do in order to run an audiobook business. Cory had considerable experience with music production, so he figured recording one person reading a book would be simple compared to mixing a band full of instruments. He already had partitioned part of his three-car garage into a recording studio, and as we modified that small area to accommodate voiceover work, he uttered what became a four-year running joke: "How hard can it be?"

Really hard. And that was just the recording part. When you're recording a thunderous rock band, the drummer and bass player could both fart holes in their pants and no one listening would notice. But stick an audiobook narrator in a six-foot-by-eight-foot room engineered to be dead silent, and you can hear a parasite licking its chops in his gut. Our first few books were less than noteworthy.

It was also really hard to make money running our own business. In fact, as I think back on my time as an entrepreneur, I believe it helped set the stage for the difficult task of downsizing for the 100 Thing Challenge. Entrepreneurs have to sacrifice a lot of stuff for the sake of their business aspirations. Leanne was supportive. And she often showed her loving support by finding creative ways to cook rice and beans. There were times in the first couple years of ChristianAudio when we literally didn't have enough money. There were times when we sold things to pay bills. I sold my nice Cannondale mountain bike for $1,000 on eBay, which helped us pay our mortgage one month.

Our business idea, however, was sound, so it outlasted the inevitable first few rough years. In the four and a half years that I helped start and grow the company, we turned it into a respected publisher of two hundred religious titles that other publishers had overlooked for the audiobook market. ChristianAudio became the leading online source of downloadable audiobooks in the Christian market. And, like most entrepreneurs, we had quite a bit of fun.

But as ChristianAudio came into its own as a company, some changes occurred that reminded me of the relentless nature of American-style consumerism. We brought on another business partner who invested a good amount of money. He had the business sense and the drive to help ChristianAudio get over the hurdle of starting up and become an established company. Without him, I'm not sure that the company would have made it. He had gone through that process a couple times before with previous companies he owned, and he came with abundant knowledge and unstoppable resolve to make ChristianAudio work. In fact, no hurdle was going to slow him down, and everything was a hurdle. But if he couldn't get over it, he was content to crash through it. Rest and patience needed to be surmounted in a never-ending sprint to "more and more."

I recognize that some people will read this as a critique of me. I was not able to live the life of an entrepreneur—after all, an entrepreneur must be relentless. "You're either growing or you're dying" is a common business mantra. Growth in profits of two or three percent is seen as failure. I disagreed with this attitude. Whether I agreed or not was beside the point. I was working with other people at my company and in my industry who felt like "more and more" was gospel truth. There came a time when I realized that I had not made peace with the fact that entrepreneurs never rest. In fact, I began to think that, if entrepreneurs never rest, then entrepreneurialism isn't a vocation for me.

A person cannot be working and resting at the same time. I am not saying that work should be restful. I am not advocating some kind of lazy man's business model in which workers never tire because their jobs are like a cozy nap. There are people who work harder and smarter than me. But in my professional career I have worked plenty of full days, late nights, and weekends. I've given up personal leisure, sacrificed time with family, and risked our finances on business opportunities. I'm a big advocate of hard work. What I am saying is that the 100 Thing Challenge caused me to think about everything in my life, not just "things."

Through the 100 Thing Challenge, I asked myself how owning too much stuff was affecting my life. I could not resist using that same formula to question other areas of my life. How was working too much affecting my life? Was I working more but getting less out of life?

And it went beyond asking about the number of hours I worked. Just like I looked at all the things I owned and kept in my closet and garage and asked, "Why? Why do I own all this stuff and what good is it doing in my life?" I also looked at my motivations for owning a business and working so many hours and asked, "Why? Why am I knocking myself out and what good is it doing for my life?"

The main reason a person looks for a new job or starts a new company is purpose. Everyone wants to feel like his or her work is making a difference. For several years at my dad's technology company I worked as a recruiter. Recruiters talk about this all the time. Studies have shown that the number one motivation for a person to leave a job is because he feels like he is not making a difference in his current position. Money is important, but for most people (and certainly for the best people), money isn't the primary motive for their work.

I agreed to join Cory in starting ChristianAudio because my dad's technology company, though successful with clients and generous to employees, didn't prioritize making a meaningful difference in the world. I made really good money there. But I spent a lot of time in front of the mirror in our bedroom trying to see if I could justify what I was doing. Over time I just couldn't look at myself and feel good about what I was accomplishing. So I became an entrepreneur with intentions to start and run a purposeful company.

But here's something remarkable I learned in my own entrepreneurial circumstance. The more that ChristianAudio grew, the more money we made, the more market share we acquired, the more industry recognition that we gained, well, the more I wanted *more*. It got harder to make the decision to turn down a publishing opportunity for a Christian romance novel just because such books were outside of our purpose. In fact, from day one we had said that the burgeoning Christian romance novel market was off-limits. It was what ChristianAudio was not. It was our distinction that we did not publish romance novels. But the more the company grew, the more my capacity grew to rationalize away our original vision for the company. Sure, I told myself, we do publish thoughtful titles and always will publish them, but we'll just publish a few mass-market "popular" audiobooks as well, so we can actually make some money.

Now please read this carefully. I want to share something with you about myself, about my mind and heart. Remember, I'm not making the case for some kind of altruistic business model here. That's for other, more qualified authors. I am telling you about what happened to me when I was an entrepreneur. As ChristianAudio became larger and as I began to focus on more and more growth for the company, my mind and heart shifted. I started thinking not only of the growth of the company, but of my own growth as a businessman. And my own growing desire for material possessions that a growing businessman could acquire.

A few years after we started our company, my business partners and I were approached by another company interested in buying ChristianAudio. We had some dialogue with them, ran through some numbers, and then put the ball in their court to come up with an offer. That week my business partners and I had a long drive up to Ventura, California, to meet with a potential distributor for our audiobooks. In the car we talked and argued about how much the inquiring company might be willing to pay for ChristianAudio. I was the positive thinker of the trio and came up with the largest figure. Also, in my mind I probably came up with the largest list of things I was going to buy with all that money. A new car. Not a luxury sedan or anything like that. In fact, I fantasized about getting a used Subaru. But a nice used Subaru. And I thought about being able to afford another dog because I would really like to have two dogs instead of one. And more adventure gear, like a solo four-season tent and a larger backpack and crampon-compatible boots and crampons and an ice axe (though I'd have had to figure out how to use it) and several kinds of jackets for all sorts of weather scenarios and other adventure gear like that. And binoculars to replace the ones I had sold years ago. And a really powerful telescope, large enough to spot the tiniest variable star. And star-map software to help me position the telescope. And a flashlight with a red-light filter so that I could see my telescope on pitch-black nights without dilating my pupils, because red light doesn't cause pupils to dilate. And a new digital SLR camera and a few really expensive lenses. And a tripod made out of basalt, which is what some really light, sturdy, and expensive tripods are made out of. And maybe some land and a small cabin in a really dark state like Nevada, or, if we made enough money to be able to afford flying instead of driving, maybe a beautiful state like Montana. And maybe a twenty- to twenty-five-foot fishing boat that I could use to fish but also to learn to navigate the ocean in preparation for getting a fifty-plus-foot ocean going trawler someday. And maybe a gun to defend against pirates and for target practice. And lots more books, because people who own weapons but don't read literature are dangerous.

Here is a rut that I've fallen into and have had a hard time working my way out of in my own life. I will not say that it's guaranteed that everyone will get stuck in this same ditch, if their lives are similar to mine. though I've known other people who seemed to trudge alongside me while I was in it. It's the rut of more and more. For some remarkable reason that I do not fully understand, more almost always makes me desire more. And more of one thing often makes me desire more of another. American-style consumerism and the entrepreneurial life I experienced both fostered this attitude of more and more in my life. The 100 Thing Challenge was my answer to feeling stuck in stuff. In the same months I thought up and prepared for my challenge, I decided that entrepreneurialism, or at least the kind of entrepreneurialism I was living, wasn't a fit for me and I sold my equity position in ChristianAudio.

I have come to believe that contentment is a virtue we can aspire to rather than a state we can achieve.

Who is the satisfied person? The person who has it all? The person who has done it all? The person who has gone further than anyone else and gotten more than anyone else? There is no such person. Of course not. We all know that. But try going to the mall and *believing* that. Try starting up a business that becomes financially successful and *believing* that. In the heat of the moment it's not so easy to remember that contentment is an attitudinal choice, not a buyable product.

My own experience—perhaps my own weakness—has proven to me that if left to my own devices, I will gravitate to more and more. Without intervention, I will not stop trying to achieve satisfaction by way of purchase or by way of work. My natural inclination is to go after satisfaction. But there's no way I can get the fulfillment I want. I go after more and more unless

I decide to rest, content in what joys can be mine. And at a certain point that's what I did: I said stop.

When I decided to sell my position in the audiobook business I said stop to the more and more of the entrepreneurial imperative. And when I came up with the 100 Thing Challenge, it was my way of pushing back against the (almost) unstoppable force of American-style consumerism.

3. "American-Style Consumerism" Got My Attention

Even if my decision to undertake the 100 Thing Challenge was somewhat spur-of-the-moment, the realization that I was in thrall to stuff did not come to me as a bolt from the blue. For some time I had been grappling with the negative effects of our consumer culture—the fact that we, when considered both as individuals and together, are defined in so many ways by material possessions and their accumulation. I knew I wanted to be free of the pressure that comes with owning so many things. But it was hard for me to put my finger on what I was freeing myself from.

It was easier for me to define what I wasn't against. Being opposed to consumerism doesn't mean, as some may think, that you don't want to buy anything, that you're even against personal possessions and money, period. Did I want to live in a prehistoric commune and barter my way through life? No.

I'm a fan of modern amenities. In reaching a definition for my malaise it was useful to parse the phrase "American-style consumerism." I found it insightful to reach for the dictionary definition of the word "consumer." Today, it has mostly benign connotations. We are, as shoppers and buyers, consumers. We talk about consumers' rights. The word is pretty much synonymous with someone who buys something.

The original definition was quite different. The *Oxford English Dictionary*'s first meaning of "consumer" is "He who or that which consumes, wastes, squanders, or destroys." Indeed, the earliest meaning was "squanderer." It's true to say that much of what we casually consume (that is, buy) we actually consume (or destroy). Take the coffee cups I threw away at Peet's Coffee while doing research for this book. The cups are not recyclable and so I quite literally "consume" them by my use. Many products like this are consumed (destroyed) when used.

On the other hand, the word "product" comes from the Latin *pro* (forth) and *ducere* (to lead). The idea is that to make something is "to lead or bring forth" something. A product is literally a creation, a making. This is not all just wordplay. These definitions are helpful. So it is entirely valid to understand our modern economic system as one that creates stuff (products) in order to consume (destroy) them.

If I wasn't going to opt out of this system entirely, or "drop out," then I was going to have to regulate my own involvement in it. I decided that it wasn't consumption per se that was my issue, it was *over*consumption—which implies that the problem is consuming more than is necessary. Even that is problematic. Because, as I've learned, overconsumption is more the norm than a deviation from it. One does not necessarily need to overconsume to do damage by consumerism. This is especially true of a person's spiritual and emotional well-being. But it is a good place to start.

This is where the "American-style" qualifier comes in. A basic tenet of our consumer culture is that we will overconsume. We will not only buy more than we strictly need (other than food, how much of what we buy do we actually need?), we will buy more than we really want. We're persuaded we want a new kitchen or car or laptop but once we've bought it, are we any happier or more fulfilled than we had been with the earlier model? Does it help when we buy into whatever new "lifestyle" is being sold to us? In my view, dissatisfaction is implicit in the fabric of consumerism. We're one big country of retail malcontents.

This is a system that we have to participate in for it to flourish. If we were all merely bystanders, the system would have to adjust to survive. I decided I could do something about it, not by trying to change the system but by changing my own role in it. I'd stop being a purchasing dolt. I wanted to be more free, less burdened, and more joyful. The exact opposite of what product marketers contend as they sell us their wares promising that if we buy, we'll be less restricted, less encumbered, happier. The way I figured it, the marketers are wrong.

Let me try to explain what I mean. I'll tell you about what was once one of my favorite outfits to wear back in the days when I worked in corporate America.

Years ago I owned two pairs of nice wool dress slacks from the upscale retailer Nordstrom. They were the same cut, just different colors: one pair was brown and the other black. I always felt good wearing them, with just one exception. Whenever I sat down the abundant gusset jutted up as if I were hiding a whale's penis behind my zipper. No doubt, shock jocks and other insecure, size-crazed men would have been delighted. Yet I am content and modest, so I felt embarrassed.

In business meetings, people would give me double and triple takes. It got to the point where I practiced sitting down and tamping my crotch with my elbow while crossing my legs in one understated motion. That worked for a time, but shift or cross my legs the other way and *whoosh*!

At the same time I owned the dress slacks, I had a belt with a silver buckle and outward-facing stitching on the leather that gave it a professional yet up-to-date look. The belt went well with the brown pair of pants, except that the belt was one size too large. Moreover, the belt loops on the pants were too small, being made for older-style, skinny suit belts. This meant that after I buckled the belt, the excess length could not fit back through the belt loop immediately to the left of the zipper. The remaining portion of the belt flopped around awkwardly. I would hold it steady between my forearm and my hip, putting my left hand in my pocket in the effort to be casual about it.

The shirt I liked to wear with these pants and belt was a very expensive cotton dress shirt I found on a great sale at an outlet mall. The shirt was silver-blue. The material was slightly thicker than most nice shirts, but it wasn't stiff or itchy and it was definitely well made. The trouble was that the shirt cuffs had no buttons—just empty buttonholes that needed filling with cuff links, which I did not have (and would not have wanted to wear anyway). I usually made do by wearing the shirt with the cuffs dangling open, making my already skinny wrists look like toothpicks wrapped in napkins.

The shoes that went best with the pants, belt, and shirt were a pair of European slip-ons. They were brown and had outward-facing stitching, like the belt, and they complemented the outfit

just right. The shoes were casual enough to fit my noncorpo-
rate demeanor, yet they were still professional. It's just that the
shoes had absolutely no arch support, and after wearing them
all day the bottoms of my feet would ache like they had been
beaten with an icing spatula.

This ensemble was a favorite outfit to wear to the office
when I was making a little less or a little more than $100,000
a year working for my dad's technology consulting firm, which
I did for about six years in a row. That casual yet stylish attire
exactly fit the successful business persona I wanted to create for
myself as I attempted to establish my career.

Or I should put it this way: if all those clothes actually fit
and functioned properly, then that outfit would have been my
ideal.

My old work getup is a metaphor for what I call American-
style consumerism. We acquire possessions that are just barely
but not quite exactly right. But we behave as if all of our consumer intentions and purchases can come together to create a
nearly perfect life. The trouble is that no store keeps ultimate
contentment in its inventory. We cannot buy what we need for
an ideal life in stores, so we have become habitual shoppers
who come up short again and again and therefore have to head
back for more. American-style consumerism encourages us to
go to a store and pick out the best of the best, but it also plants
a seed of doubt in our minds. The disappointment is built in.
When we get home we decide that what we just bought may not
be the best of the best, and so we put it in our closet or in our
garage and go back to a store and get something else that we
think is going to be the best of the best.

. . .

As I was arranging my thoughts about consumerism, I found myself returning to the subject of dreams, and two dreams in particular. One was a dream of mine, the other a dream seemingly shared by the collective American unconscious.

For almost thirty years I have remained fascinated by a dream I had one morning as a nine-year-old child. The dream was complicated, included many characters from my waking life, spanned several decades, and ended with something awkward happening to my foot (exactly what, I don't recall). When I awoke it was still dark behind the curtains of my bedroom window and my dad was shaking my real foot to get me up for a trout fishing trip. That very moment, I marveled at the speed with which our minds work as I instantly processed what had just happened. In the couple of dozen seconds it took my father to jiggle my foot to wake me, my soul abstracted an entire lifetime experience that culminated perfectly in an improbable foot-shaking plot twist.

Now, three decades later, I couldn't help thinking I'd woken up again. Just like before, the "dream" was complicated and a lot of time seemed to have passed. Again, it took only a moment, once awake, to take it all in. Only this time my dad wasn't directly involved and there was no intrigue surrounding my foot. I felt as if I had been jolted alert by the foolishness of American-style consumerism, and it was my soul that had been shaken awake. Rather than rubbing the sleep from my eyes to go fishing, in the summer of 2007, I freaked out and got rid of most of my personal belongings. I named my waking madness the 100 Thing Challenge.

It was a short leap, for my literal-minded brain, from that dream to the next one. Significant in our national mythology is the notion of the American dream. This dream often refers to the success of immigrants who, once they achieve a level of prosperity and security, are said to be living the American dream. As Americans, we're either living the dream, or aspiring to live it, depending on where we are in life. I believe the stereotypical notion of the American dream is inexcrably tied up with American-style consumerism, usually coming on the heels of material want and achieved by hard work. Most often, the dream's plateau coincides with a perceived threshold of stuff accumulation. I will never deny anyone the right to aspire to something more, even if it's just more stuff. I do think, however, that associating this desire with a "dream" is highly misleading.

Consider what we actually dream about when we are asleep. It's a lot more weird stuff—soaring through the air, running from a predator—than it is BMWs or nice watches. Everyone's dreams are extremely personal and unique to them. They are often strange and incoherent; Leanne's certainly seem to be when she describes them to me. Sometimes she'll wake me up to recount something particularly unusual. I'm rarely in Leanne's dreams; she's in mine even less frequently. It's certainly never happened that we have woken up and discovered we were having the same dream. But unlike our individual nighttime dreams, the parameters of what supposedly make up our mass desires, and what we need to obtain to be living the American dream, are remarkably similar. And so the point I am getting at through all of this is that the American dream, when compared to what our actual dreams are like, is more of a fantasy, a consumer fantasy, that is ultimately out of our reach.

Also, and this is key, while we dream alone, we consume together. This so-called dream life is something that a husband would be expected to share with his wife and family. You wouldn't expect a wife to be living the American dream while her husband and kids are not. The paradigm doesn't work like that. (It's another reason why a fantasy—always a solitary creation—is a better description than a dream.) American-style consumerism is a group activity, the key word here being "activity." Again, it's something that is maintained by our active participation. If we actually left consumerism to our dreams, it would wither away.

Leanne and I often shop together. We went to Pier 1 Imports to buy the bed that we sleep and dream in. Granted, through the years, we have had a difference of opinion about duvet covers. I like warm solid colors and masculine patterns like stripes. She is attracted to paisley and floral motifs. Even so, we have always come to some form of reconciliation when we purchase one. Together we picked out the carpet for our bedroom flooring. By this same accord we decided on the bamboo flooring in our living room and the tile in our kitchen. And so it has been with most of our household purchases.

What's more, I have observed that we are far from the only couple that engages in joint consuming. Right from the get-go of our marriage I noticed that consuming is a social activity. Back when we went to Crate & Barrel to create our wedding registry, there were other couples just like us, anxiously mulling over silverware and place settings and contemplating couches, wondering if it would be presumptuous to add a thousand-dollar item to their wish list. The store was packed full of stuff and couples buying stuff.

That scene—a crowded store filled with thousands of products and dozens of people—represents the very nature of American-style consumerism. It is a collective activity. Consumerism cannot be done alone. And American-style consumerism, the kind of consumerism that is relentlessly pressing for more stuff, cannot even be done merely in tandem. It requires masses of participants. On this point, in her excellent book *A Consumers' Republic*, Lizabeth Cohen quotes the liberal economist Robert R. Nathan, who was unstinting in his efforts to mobilize manufacturing in post–World War II America. Nathan believed that the United States needed to produce more things in order to grow more affluent. But he also understood that those things needed to be bought. "Ever-increasing consumption," he said, "on the part of our people [is] one of the prime requisites for prosperity. Mass consumption is essential to the success of a system of mass production.'*

When I walked around my house on that July day in 2007 contemplating all of my stuff, I felt like living proof of Nathan's thesis. For nearly forty years I had upheld my part of the bargain, doing what I could to mass-consume. And I expect that our house and my life would have appeared successful to most people looking in. Except how do we define "prosperity"? Is prosperity only a material condition? Is there not prosperity of the soul? Outward riches without inward peace, I think we can all agree, is a tentative state of wealth.

Since World War II, under the influence of economists and policy makers like Nathan, American-style consumerism has brought prosperity that can be seen on the outside. Mass consumption in the United States is now ubiquitous. Habitual shopping has become *the* measure of affluence for individuals as well as whole regions. Prosperity must be displayed or else it will be in doubt. *Newsweek* editor Robert Samuelson says that post–Second World War Americans shopped their way out of economic turmoil through "mass suburbanization and a prodi-

---

* Lizabeth Cohen, *A Consumers' Republic* (New York: Alfred A. Knopf, 2003), 116.

gious outpouring of consumer goods." Comparing the circumstances of the 1950s to today's recession, Samuelson says, "So
much of our national identity is wrapped up in economic progress that the failure to achieve it in palpable quantities would
sap America's self-confidence."*

But consumerism isn't only an outward measure of national
well-being. Over the years I have found myself thinking that the
quantity and quality of *my* personal possessions is a measure of
my inward contentment. I want a self-confident life filled with
satisfaction. In that pursuit I have found that creature comfort
is hard to pass up. So is a great deal at the mall. I have mixed
physical ease with material possessions. I have been chasing
after a life that seems filled with greater and greater possibilities. And I have tried to get there by what I have purchased at
stores. And when I have gotten enough comfort and stuff, as
the dominant cultural tale tells me, then I really will be living
my American dream.

Yet there are consequences to this pattern of striving for
more stuff as a means of gaining more satisfaction. It turns
many of us who participate in the cycle of American-style consumerism not into satisfied people, but into narcissistic jack-
asses. Despite the inescapable shared nature of consumerism,
when I read Bill McKibben's words—"The very act of acquiring
so much stuff has turned us ever more into individuals and
ever less into members of a community, isolating us in a way
that runs contrary to our most basic instincts"†—they stung
even as they rang true to my individual experience,

If you want to understand the connection between personal

---

* Robert Samuelson, "A Darker Future for Us," *Newsweek*, November 10, 2008.
† Bill McKibben, *Deep Economy: The Wealth of Communities and the Durable Future*
(New York: Times Books, 2007), 37.

possessions and relationships, go to a person who has neither. What is the attitude of a castaway? Alone on an island she has no one around her and nothing of her own. Of all people on earth, the castaway ought to feel like the center of the universe. But without industry and its branded products she instead becomes the least selfish person alive. Every thought and action reminds her of the stuff she does not have and the people she cannot see. Possessing no hand mirror, her eyes are always on the horizon. Her philosophy is all about the possibilities beyond herself. But rescue her and bring her back home, and her ideology changes. Give her all she needs, wants, and more. Take away the sea-filled horizon and put her on Fifth Avenue in New York City. Let her shop with credit cards. Soon enough you will see her emerge from a store oblivious, coddling her latest best-of-the-best purchase by herself, even in the midst of the rabble of consumerism all around her.

That is an uncomfortable picture. American-style consumerism has created a mob of people rushing to acquire ever more stuff. But the riffraff in the crowd don't seem to notice each other.

Maybe you feel differently than I do. Too often in my life I have been a heedless participant in the ruckus of consumerism. I have bought stuff my family could not afford, knowing the expense would stress out my wife, recognizing all the while that the thing was not going to make me happy. Confession: the rock climbing wall at the back of the garage that cost a good $200 in materials? Well, it didn't make me into a rock climber and it didn't satisfy my longings for adventure. Like so many other purchases, the rock climbing wall ultimately was more of an expense and distraction than it was a pleasure.

We're so distracted, we're missing our own lives. The parent who records his kid's dance recital or first steps or graduation is so busy trying to capture the moment—to create a thing that proves they were there—they miss out on actually living and enjoying the moment.

I've done this before with my camera. I have jockeyed for position, bumping elbows with other parents so I could get into the best spot to look through the viewfinder of my SLR to capture the moment of my daughter's dance recital. Five-year-old Phoebe was so cute in her little sailor outfit, tapping away. And I got some great pictures. It's just that while I remember getting the pictures, I do not recall the moment. So much of the time we don't trust ourselves to experience our world without stuff. Things so often don't enhance our lives, but are barriers to fully *living* our lives.

. . .

I have been caught up in these distractions even when my intention was otherwise. I have told my parents that I have all that I need and asked them not to give me gifts, only to receive more birthday or Christmas presents than normal. Ungrateful though it sounds, many of those gifts have been a strain on me. I do not know what to do with them or where to put them or how, graciously, to get rid of them. And, whether by my own weakness or by the power of possessions, over the years quite a few of those gifts have worked on my mind like sirens driving me crazy for more, more, more. I'm given a fancy pen, then I start appreciating and desiring fancier pens. I'm given a gift card for a couple hundred dollars to the Home Depot, then I start browsing magazine articles about home remodeling projects that cost thousands of dollars. I have struggled with these things in my mind all by myself. Or so I thought.

I am not a castaway on an island. When family and friends know that Dave likes collecting fancy pens, my little consumer hobby is no longer a private matter. When a house project turns into a multithousand-dollar "improvement," a once welcoming home becomes a two-thousand-square-foot battlefield in the never-ending war of suburban tit for tat.

All this unsettled me. It is the reason that the 100 Thing Challenge, which might sound trivial or exhibitionist to some, was itself actually very uncomfortable to me. It functioned in my life like an attention-grabbing shout over the noisy throng of American-style consumerism. But when I decided I no longer wanted to have an abundance of stuff, a lot of things I didn't want to know about myself became clear along with the shelves in my closet. And I had to admit that in spite of my desire and my public stand against mass consumerism on my blog, I was smack dab in the middle of its chaos.

I had to look around and evaluate an ugly scene in which I was playing a supporting role.

So what did I see? I think sociologist Juliet Schor has the right vision and has interpreted American-style consumerism precisely in her marvelous book *The Overspent American*. What's more, she figured it out in the late 1990s. Before the dot-com bubble burst. Before the subprime mortgage meltdown. Before the collapse of Wall Street. Before the Great Recession that began in December 2007. Before all the twenty-first-century economic ills that caused me to doubt our excessive consumer behavior. She said of Americans what has personally rung true of me, "We are impoverishing ourselves in pursuit of a consumption goal that is inherently unachievable."*

---

* Juliet Schor, *The Overspent American* (New York: Basic Books, 1998), 109.

Not only are our bank accounts and businesses and government and the environment drained, but also our souls as we try to purchase the American dream.

"All the toil of man is for his mouth, yet his appetite is not satisfied," wrote wise King Solomon thousands of years before Schor repeated his erudition. From the beginning of time immemorial sages have recognized the insufficiency of stuff to conciliate our deepest cravings.

Here's the bottom line: what we really want we cannot buy.

4. Every Challenge Needs Rules

After I took stock of my situation, it was clear to me that I was caught in this cycle of American-style consumerism. Even though I didn't want to be, I was stuck in the habit of consuming for contentment that only left me dissatisfied. The 100 Thing Challenge was a spontaneous idea that seemed like a doable scheme to help me get unstuck. But if it was going to work, I actually needed a plan. I needed rules.

When overused, rules can put a damper on life. Yet rules are a necessary condition of reality. Perhaps you have noticed that the fantasy life promoted by American-style consumerism doesn't seem to follow rules. It's a free-for-all (except it isn't free). One moment you are anxiously staring at your underfunded checkbook, the next you're swiping a credit card at Pottery Barn, crossing your fingers that you'll find a way in the future to pay for the new curtains, which you hope will make your bedroom more inviting, which you hope will help you get along with your spouse, who is stressed to the breaking point because, even with two incomes, the two of you cannot pay for all your stuff. Dream on. The 100 Thing Challenge was designed to be my alarm clock.

By the end of July I had formulated a strategy to make this happen. Here is how I planned to wake myself up. For one year, from November 12, 2008, my thirty-seventh birthday, to November 12, 2009, my thirty-eighth birthday, I was going to live with only one hundred personal possessions. I figured I could knock myself awake and out of the pattern of American-style consumerism by removing myself from the possibility of taking part in it. Yet I realized that I and this new project of mine needed more than just time. My experiment away from consumerism needed some boundaries. This is where the rules came in.

It's one thing to make a spontaneous decision. It's a whole other thing altogether to sit down and think about the choices we make. When those choices begin to affect family members, well . . . I mean, what was going to qualify as a "personal possession"? Was I going to end up downsizing possessions that I thought I no longer needed but that my wife felt perfectly comfortable keeping? What about sentimental items? Is it worth selling priceless family heirlooms on eBay to make a point about the worthless trinkets of today's consumerism? What kind of message does that send to my family and even the wider community around me?

And then there's the practical nature of twenty-first-century possessions. Would I count digital objects in addition to material objects? And how would I satisfy those reality-TV-trained naysayers who surely would nitpick that my pair of trail running shoes with laces are not one separate thing but *four*, two shoes and two laces, not one?

. . .

First things first: Why one hundred things? One hundred is an ordinary number. It sounds familiar, and yet it is still kind of impressive. That is why I picked one hundred for my possessions limit. There is nothing mysterious about the number, though when I was young, a one-hundred-dollar bill was nearly magical, almost mythical. In grade school, typing one plus one on my calculator and then tapping the equals button ninety-nine times could take up a noticeable amount of class. And it did. Many times. In a row. Which might help explain why I repeated first grade, but I digress.

The point is that I like one hundred. 100. It is a good number. It is bigger than one. I have found over the years that it is fairly easy to sign a petition . . . once. It is pretty simple to exercise . . . once. I can say I am sorry . . . once. But once a habit does not make. Once a meaningful lifestyle does not create.

Numbers can be overwhelming, though. The world has roughly 143,000,000 orphans. There are more than 2,000,000,000 people living in poverty. There is $13,000,000,000,000,000 of U.S. government debt, according to usdebtclock.org. Those numbers are too big for me to handle. But I can get my mind around one hundred. Even so, one hundred is not a get-off-easy number. Let me tell you, it isn't simple to live in modern America with only one hundred personal things. It'll get your attention. It's a challenge. But one hundred is also obtainable. A 10 Thing Challenge wouldn't work for me, nor anyone living anything other than the life of a hermit. And larger numbers would be too easy: a thousand things is hardly a challenge at all. One hundred things proved to be just right—it was hard to achieve but not impossible, difficult to maintain but not infeasible. A challenge should be something that is within your abilities, however stretched, to complete; otherwise it's just an ordeal or a trial. Besides (see Rule Number One), it was my number to pick.

Rule Number One: It's Dave's Challenge

I realized that as I began to formulate the details of the 100 Thing Challenge, I was not merely coming up with regulations for myself. I was also creating the context in which people—my family and friends and community, and even strangers—would interpret and respond to my project. Of course the people most directly affected would be my family.

The plan for the 100 Thing Challenge never included the direct participation of my wife and daughters. Rule Number One was that the 100 Thing Challenge was my personal effort and not something I was going to force onto anyone else, my family most of all. Of course, they would be dragged along on my journey to some extent, since living with another family member's choices is a consequence of living with another family member.

Rule Number Two: Defining "Personal Things"

Personal things are things that are entirely or mostly mine. Clearly, family-shared and household items (for example, a dining room table, piano, bed, plates, and so on) are not considered personal things.

If Rule Number One established that the 100 Thing Challenge was my burden, then Rule Number Two needed to establish what exactly were my personal possessions that had created the burden of consumerism in my life. My 100 Thing Challenge wasn't about purging our daughters' toys (we'll come to that knotty issue in the next chapter). Likewise, my efforts to live without an abundance of things wasn't meant to infringe on Leanne's desire to live with whatever was hers or whatever she saw fit to own for our household. So what, exactly, is a "personal possession"?

On the surface that is an easy question to answer. My underwear, for example, is mine. Leanne would never dare to borrow my skivvies, nor would she care to. And, though I have heard about other men who don't feel the same way, I would never dream of donning a pair of Leanne's intimates. Occasionally Leanne has worn one of my shirts around the house or grabbed one of my jackets in a frantic rush to get out of the door. Those rare instances, however, when what is clearly my possession gets shared with my wife, did not seem to me like justification that any of my clothing items were "shared" things. All of my clothes were my stuff and should be treated like my personal possessions for the 100 Thing Challenge. I would require myself to count my clothes.

Other items seemed to be all mine, too. I am an avid thinker and writer who keeps a journal full of ideas for my next great business start-up or book story line and doodles. Leanne and I have been married for fourteen years. As far as I am aware, she has never read through my journals without my consent. And even if she has (come to think of it, I wonder if she has?), such behavior on her part wouldn't negate the fact that something so individual and supposedly private as a journal is clearly a personal possession. I counted my journal as one thing. Further, I counted the blue mechanical pencil that I used to write in my journal as one thing. As far as it was within my power, I determined to use only that pencil for any pencil-writing needs for the entire year.

My clothes. My journal. My one pencil. I also kept one pen because I usually do the bills and it's best to write checks in ink. Some of the other things that clearly seemed to be all mine included my wedding ring, wallet, watch, cell phone, car, toothbrush, razor (though I questioned the decision to count the razor a few times when the blade painfully bounced down my cheek, having been dulled unbeknownst to me by rapid swipes across Leanne's legs), adventure gear, and a number of electronic items. My Apple laptop I counted as mine. I also put the Apple iMac that is in our bedroom on my 100 Thing Challenge list. In retrospect, that was probably a mistake. I used that computer almost never. But at the time I counted my possessions, it seemed better to be safe than hypocritical.

Strict though I tried to be, I came to find that cautious imprecision has a subjective side. Trying to determine the specifics of my personal possessions got fuzzy the more things I counted. Our bed, for example, is most definitely a shared thing, though I have my side of the bed. Would I count personal territory as a thing? My place at the dinner table? My spot on the couch? If I did, for example, would my side of the bed be one full thing or a half of a thing? Since Leanne rolls over and pulls most of the blanket off me each night, would I count the comforter as only a fourth of a thing? Come nighttime when I'm in bed, my dog Piper thinks that my spot on the couch is his spot. So would I count this place on the couch as half of a spot?

After giving this some thought, I decided on two ways forward. I would count only whole things. If something was going to have to count as a half item, then it wasn't going to count. I also determined to judge whether I would count shared items like the bed or the couch by a more subjective measure. I tried to honestly ask myself if the shared thing was an item I have had consumerism problems with in my life. In fourteen years of marriage we have owned two bed frames and two mattresses. Moreover, we have switched which side of the bed we sleep on at least three times based on how we have arranged and rearranged the master bedrooms we've inhabited. The bed and my place in the bed are just not that important to me. I mostly want to sleep in our bed and frankly I don't very much care what it looks like. Though mattresses and bedroom furniture are surely a prime target for the marketers of American-style consumerism, for me (and Leanne for that matter), the bed just isn't a big deal. I wanted to break my consumer compulsions, not split hairs over shared things in our household.

If shared items weren't going to count, I still had to make some difficult choices about the things that were definitely mine.

I made four decisions that could turn people off the 100 Thing Challenge. I made four "exceptions" that definitely did not sit well with those who demand precision of others, whether or not they take such care to evaluate their own lives.

Rule Number Three: Memorabilia

To begin with, I was going to keep a small box of memorabilia. But it turned out that I don't have much. So I ditched this idea and just counted one hand-me-down Bible, a small New Testament that my dad had given me. My understanding is that he had it with him in Vietnam and that his dad carried it when he served in World War II. I've never served in the military, but somehow this Bible didn't seem like a thing I should purge. (I had two other Bibles that I kept besides this one.)

Rule Number Four: Books

Ah, here's the rub. We're avid readers in our home. And even the books I don't read thrice a year look very attractive as they collect dust on the bookshelves. And many of my books are kind of work-related. Strange as it sounds, I have a lot of history books that relate directly or indirectly to consumerism and that help me with the 100 Thing Challenge. So I decided to keep "one library."

I should pause here and mention digital media. I did have some electronic files: many pictures, some music, a handful of videos, and a few audiobooks. But I don't buy many digital products. Whether it is because I'm jejune or too scatterbrained, I don't listen to music much. For the last two years I have been commuting two hours a day to my job. I think I've listened to music no more than a dozen times. I've quietly motored along thinking for hundreds of hours, though.

My computer had a couple of U2 albums I'd purchased, the greatest hits album of the Police, and a Jack Johnson album (I do live in San Diego). It had only one movie on it that I'd bought from iTunes expressly for myself, a surfing movie that much later I was very glad I had around. It had a few episodes of the television version of *This American Life*.

I'll admit that Amazon's Kindle had tempted me, but I never bought one. I poked around Amazon.com off and on and discovered that most of the books I like to read are not available for the Kindle, so it would not be able to replace my physical library.

Digital products seem like they should be more important to me. It feels like a guy who promotes downsizing material objects as a route to simplicity should be a booster of digital stuff as a way to accomplish that. But I'm just not that guy. I wouldn't want to go a week without my Apple MacBook Pro, my blog, Facebook, Twitter, and the Internet. But, if it makes sense, I don't really care about digital things so much.

Rule Number Five: A Few Items Were Counted in Groups

This includes underwear, undershirts (not T-shirts), and socks. I did not keep a lot of either. We do, though, run a household. The idea of trying to manage laundry with only a few pairs of skivvies and socks was both unrealistic and gross.

Rule Number Six: Household Items

I decided to keep some household tools that would not go on my 100 Thing Challenge list: hammer, screwdriver, tape measure, etc. For example, after my 100 Thing Challenge started, I needed some tools to put up my daughter's gymnastics bar in a hallway. I'm not using the tools for anything more than honey-do projects. Moreover, I did part with many of my less practical tools, which I'll discuss in a later chapter.

Rule Number Seven: Gifts

I also left myself a cushion in case I received a gift or two over the course of the challenge, though I hoped that everyone who might give me a gift knew that they shouldn't! Anyway, once I received a gift, I had seven days to figure out what to do with it before it counted toward my 100 Thing Challenge. I figured that should be enough time to either graciously lose it or get rid of some other thing on my list.

Rule Number Eight: New Things

Finally, I could get new things. But I always had to remain under one hundred things total. And also if I "replaced" something, I had to get rid of the original item before I got the new one.

Once I had codified my rules, I felt ready to accept my challenge. I was happy with the way the rules worked out. The rules were such that neither success nor failure was predetermined. Nor was I making life unnecessarily onerous for my family. I felt that with some luck and a lot of support and a certain amount of willpower, I could live with one hundred things for a year. But there was something I had to do first. I had to get down to one hundred things.

5. Personal Change Begins at Home

The decision to make the 100 Thing Challenge my personal project and not a family mandate proved a good one a couple months into purging my personal belongings to get myself ready for my year of living with less. Leanne and I took the momentum I was gaining in my clean up efforts and used it as inspiration for the whole family. We asked our daughters to downsize their American Girl dolls and accessories collections, not as a hard-and-fast attempt to get them to participate in the 100 Thing Challenge, but simply in the spirit of encouraging them to get into the habit of removing the excess stuff in their lives.

Our policy for American Girl dolls and accessories always had been straightforward. Keep it simple. Leanne and I both like the American Girl products. The dolls themselves are costly, but not exorbitant. The accessories are well crafted and enjoyable for our girls (and even us) to play with. The novels that place each of the American Girl dolls into historical context are excellent, introducing children not only to important eras in American history but also addressing complex themes of virtue in the midst of nuanced life choices. And though there are people who will no doubt disagree with me on this point, I appreciate what seems like the restraint that the American Girl company has shown by not placing a store in every mall. (Yes, I know American Girl, LLC, is a subsidiary of the evil toy behemoth Mattel and that Mattel is sneaking American Girl products into new distribution channels, but this is a recent development.) There are only a handful of American Girl shops around the country. I suspect they could open more and make more money. Limiting the number of stores surely makes the brand a luxury, but it also makes a statement against profusion. The point is that Leanne and I believe that all young girls should experience the joy of playing with dolls, and the American Girl dolls, all things considered, seemed like a good fit for us.

So early in our daughters' lives we put a doll plan into action. Each of our girls would get a Bitty Baby doll sometime between their first and second birthdays. Bitty Baby is the "baby" American Girl. She comes with footsie pajamas and her own tiny stuffed animal, Bitty Bear. She's not grown up like the others, but she makes an excellent first doll. Once our girls themselves grew up a bit more, each of them would get one more American Girl and some accessories to accompany her. That was our plan.

Our intentions, however, were confounded by an unstoppable consumer force: grandmas. If I have any suspicion of marketing connivance on the part of American Girl, it is not that they trick children into a lifestyle of consumption but rather that they hoodwink grandmothers into a binge of gift buying. To be fair, what grandmother could resist? Certainly not Leanne's mom or mine. The long and short of it is that within a couple years of putting our American Girl plan into action, our home looked like an overbooked hostel for adorable foot-tall girls with unkempt hair. There wasn't a place we could avoid tripping over one of those little sweethearts.

So on a benign day in the fall of 2007 Leanne and I sent Lucy and Phoebe and Bridget into their rooms to select which American Girl dolls they could do without. It seemed like a reasonable request of them. Then we went about our own house cleaning business. After a couple of hours, no daughters or American Girls had emerged from the rooms. I wondered if perhaps they were taking the spirit of the 100 Thing Challenge to heart and delighting in the freedom of letting go of their stuff. I felt proud that my 100 Thing Challenge was setting such a great example for my daughters and that they were rising above the consumer indulgence all around them. I went to find them in their rooms and congratulate them with a smile on my face.

With the same fortitude and obedience that Abraham had shown when he tied Isaac to the altar and lifted his knife high into the air, our girls had consigned a few of their American Girl dolls to boxes intended for charity. But the boxes were graves. And our daughters had murderer-tears streaming down their faces. Phoebe had actually put her doll into the box facedown because she could not bear to look at its face. I had trouble looking into her face, too. As God spared Abraham, I too relented (only without omnipotence and the foresight of redemption) and called out for my daughters to stop. They could keep their dolls and the real relationships they nurtured with them in their imaginations.

On that day I learned an important lesson about personal decisions. Keep them personal. I cannot say that I never had fantasies of the 100 Thing Challenge turning into a revolution in which the masses rise up and put the kibosh on American-style consumerism for good. Perhaps the 100 Thing Challenge would engender changed attitudes across America about what constitutes affluence and economic prosperity. The temptations to think this way, though, are the selfish fancies that so often lure me into delusions of grandeur. They are the temptations to see myself in God's place as the mediator of providence. It was said, "The heart of man plans his way, but the Lord establishes his steps." (Proverbs 16:9) If I cannot even manage my own destiny without some divine help, surely I cannot expect to change the economy of the United States singlehandedly.

A primary objective of the 100 Thing Challenge was that I wanted to use the experience to chasten my own consumer behavior. It has never been my desire to constrain the actions of others. If others chose to participate, that would be fine, but it needed to be their choice. My daughters helped me appreciate the importance of this attitude. The truth is that there is no direct correlation between a young girl's loving care for her doll and a grown man's greed for ever more objects of status. When a child is forced to give away a cherished toy, it is more likely to damage her heart than build up her character. That is not the same for adults who can learn a good deal about virtue when they restrict their covetousness.

Of course I am *not* saying that teaching children temperance is unnecessary. Children do need nudges from adults in order to learn virtues. What they do not need is for parents to deal with their own faults by exacting punishing "lessons" on their kids.

One of the main reasons I came to insist on focusing the challenge on my own personal belongings was that I recognized my own immaturity in the area of possessions. I had been spending years blabbing against consumerism but had made inadequate progress toward simplicity in my own life. Who was I to place expectations on my family or other people? If I were to truly have a message, at minimum I felt I ought to get my own things in order before starting to share.

Interestingly, when I backed away from mandating consumer change for my daughters, it gave them the space they needed to become inquiring observers of the 100 Thing Challenge. No longer threatened that I might walk from my closet to theirs to purge their things, they could watch me wrestle through my decisions, processing my experience from a safe distance. Their reactions turned into curiosity, which is a foundation of healthy personal development. Instead of worrying that I might come down on them for having too many toys, they felt comfortable asking their nutty dad why he was doing the 100 Thing Challenge in the first place.

Phoebe could safely ask, "Are you going to live with only one hundred things forever?" I let her know that wasn't my plan: rather, I was trying to break my habit of seeking satisfaction through owning things. This was especially meaningful for Phoebe, because she was born with a shopping gene that has given her a disposition to want to buy her way to happiness. She's an eight-year-old who likes to buy and will do so excessively if left to her own devices. Talking with her about a big-picture life choice to prioritize more meaningful things than material possessions was a better way to instruct her than squelching her enthusiastic consumer heart.

Lucy could pull me into her confidence: "I know I shouldn't

want to buy this toy because I really don't need it, but I *do* want it." Eleven-year-old Lucy is our compliant first child who would rather break her left arm with her right than break one of our family rules. What she was really saying was "Dad, I kind of understand what you are doing, but I want to buy this cool toy with my allowance. Are you still going to like me if I do?" "Of course!" I said. But I needed to show her by my actions that I meant it. Lucy did not need rules from me explaining under what circumstances it was permissible for her to consume. She needed to know that there was something more important than thrifty fiduciary advice—namely, fatherly acceptance and love.

I cannot say I remember what Bridget did that day of doll drama. She would have had only a Bitty Baby back then. Bridget herself looks like an American Girl doll with golden hair and bright eyes, and she was (and is) full of spunk. I bet we asked her to try to find some other toy or two to give to children without so much stuff as our family had. And even if Bridget had four American Girl dolls, I don't think she would have minded getting rid of three. Since she was about two years old she has gravitated toward sharks, dragons, and other violent beasts. She likes dolls, but not with the same attachment as her sisters. Someday Bridget will be old enough to read in the book of Job how God created the monster Leviathan. I suspect that's when she'll make whatever faith she learns in our home her own personal choice.

．　．　．

My wife, Leanne, reacted to the 100 Thing Challenge differently from our daughters. She was less curious. And she was the one who instructed me.

In our household all the best family sayings come from

Leanne. Her sayings combine truth with feminine power. I can quarrel with Leanne for days and usually keep one step ahead of her in our argument through my logically cunning husband rhetoric. But as soon as she pulls out one of her sayings, I know that I'm done for. Leanne's initial reaction to the 100 Thing Challenge was to roll her suspicious eyes and wonder what her ever-entrepreneurial husband was scheming up now. It didn't take long for the 100 Thing Challenge to generate some tension in our lives, and before I knew it she had me at her mercy with her woman aphorisms.

"It's your problem and I don't have to fix it."

Look, I knew that my wife had great boundaries and was capable of keeping my responsibilities my problem, but had I known how hard the 100 Thing Challenge was going to be and how much attention it was going to generate, I would have written her involvement explicitly into the rules. I would have added Rule Number Nine: "My wife must do everything within her power to prevent me from making a fool of myself."

Yes, it was my problem that I thought up the 100 Thing Challenge and announced my intention to live with only a hundred personal possessions to the world. Yes, that meant the onus was on me to find a way to get my stuff down to one hundred things. Yes, when outsiders inquired about the 100 Thing Challenge, it was my job to say something thoughtful about living a simple lifestyle. Yes, that was all true. Yet women need to understand that in the judgment of a husband, such a delicate circumstance as I found myself in is exactly where an intelligent and compassionate wife can make her greatest contribution.

Leanne held her ground. Her firm stance that the 100 Thing Challenge was my problem to solve helped me appreciate one role wives play in a healthy marriage: ensuring their lazybones husbands take responsibility for themselves. It was not right for me to unload bags of my things at the Goodwill drop-off only to turn around and burden Leanne with the stress I was creating for myself by taking the 100 Thing Challenge. The anxiety of choosing what items to purge, finding ways to get rid of them, dealing with the pressures of suspicious family and friends, juggling media attention—all these were my obligations. Leanne wished to be a loving and supportive wife; she had no desire to be the person doing the 100 Thing Challenge. And so when things got really intense in the months before the start of the challenge on November 12, she pulled out her most cogent saying: "It's your own damn fault."

There was nowhere to hide. She was right. My dear wife was paraphrasing Rule Number One: It's Dave's Challenge, with inescapable clarity.

The truth of the matter was that almost all on my own I had gotten myself stuck in stuff. I had formed my consumer habits before Leanne and I ever met. Even though we got married young—I was twenty-four and she was twenty—I came into our marriage with plenty of things and a bent to acquire more. During the twelve years of marriage before I dreamed up the 100 Thing Challenge, Leanne had played only a minor part in my consumer choices. Perhaps over time she had encouraged me here or there to purchase something I didn't need or truly want. When several years into our life together I spent many months obsessing about buying the exact right pair of binoculars, it was she who told me, "Just get some." So I did. But if Leanne sometimes abetted my consumer choices, she often did it uninformed. "You paid more than *two hundred dollars* for binoculars?" And I cannot blame her for that. Consumers can be sneaky. I have heard of other men and women who buy stuff behind their spouses' backs.

Of all the things I bought over the years in my hopes of having a better or more interesting life, few of those possessions were interesting to her or corresponded to her hopes. The faux dream life my possessions allegedly led toward was not the real life she cared about getting to. This brings me to Leanne's most infamous saying, the one that was the most help as I dealt with both the practical matters of the 100 Thing Challenge and the stress it was generating: "Bloom where you are planted."

Just so you know, it is not my natural disposition to find contentment wherever I am. In fact, I am expert at imagining gratification in circumstances other than my own.

This is such an important point. I want to slow down as I write. Take your time to read this paragraph. What I observed about myself was that my desires to downsize my personal belongings and break free from American-style consumerism coincided with my impulse to flee. As I prepared for my 100 Thing Challenge, I wanted not only to get rid of stuff but also to get rid of my lifestyle. I wanted to get rid of my job. I wanted to get rid of my suburban locale. I fantasized not only of living with empty closets but also of living on empty land, a ranch or someplace where I could have another dog or two. A place where I could walk for ten minutes and find myself alone and I wouldn't be able to see red-tiled roofs all around me and wouldn't be able to hear the constant buzz of cars driving by me. A place where I could actually build a treehouse for my daughters, who love to climb trees and who desperately want a treehouse. A place where my wife and I could make a home away from the suffocating demands of middle-class American suburbia.

I have observed this impulse to escape in other practitioners of the simple life, too. There is a tendency among those of us who advocate for simplicity to resist settlement. We want to buck cultural trends and conformity to the system. We want to go where we want, when we want, and how we want. We want simplicity, even if it comes by means of determined escape. But I was missing a reality nearer to home that Leanne opened my eyes to. I need Leanne. We need Leannes.

In my wife's resistance to shouldering the burdens of my 100 Thing Challenge and my urge to run away from my circumstances was a discriminating insight that I had been blind to. Living a life of simplicity does not end in a life of detachment; it does not mean we have to run away. It's just the opposite. Becoming free from the confining nature of American-style consumerism wasn't a way for me to free myself from everything. It was a route for me to bond with what is more properly my place in this world. My place was not within the walls of the shopping mall, where for more than three decades I had purchased things that allegedly would aid my escape from a dull life. My place was also not the wide open world, where I might wander with a rucksack filled with only a couple dozen belongings in an effort to find myself. Living a life of simplicity, I have come to believe, is not a lonely, self-centered discipline. My place wasn't somewhere else. "All of us . . . are in some manner torn between caring and not caring, staying and going."* I belong where I am.

Leanne belongs where she is. My daughters belong where they are. All the family, friends, and strangers who took an

---

* Wendell Berry, *Another Turn of the Crank* (Washington, D.C.: Counterpoint, 1995), 69.

interest in my 100 Thing Challenge belong where they are, too. Leanne helped me appreciate that maturity is not so much about going places as it is about making places.

And so Leanne said, "Bloom where you are planted." Make the soil where you've been stuck a more beautiful place.

6. Purging Things and "Things Past"

If I was going to stay put and grow by means of my 100 Thing Challenge, so to speak, I needed to tend to my plot of land. My parcel was filled with a lot of weedlike things. Hundreds of personal possessions. Things that were interfering with the intentions of the 100 Thing Challenge and that were tangling up the blooming of my life. I needed to purge for the practical reason that narrowing my personal belongings down to one hundred was my stated purpose. Yet in the process of getting ready for the November 12 start of my challenge, I came to understand that downsizing wasn't the only way to take care of what I'd accumulated over the years. It was also going to be my way forward.

I am startled by the expectations I sometimes place on my stuff. There are times when I stare down at one of my possessions and kind of squint my eyes for a while. When I refocus and my vision becomes clear again, I want to see not only that thing but also my whole life in a new light.

My father had a collection of toy trains when I was growing up. They were German trains made by Märklin. He kept them in the closet of the extra room of our house in a huge black case made especially for storing Ho scale-model trains. The case had pullout drawers that were lined with felt and sectioned perfectly to hold the engines and cars in neat rows. I would open the case and stare at those trains for hours on end.

When I was a boy, my father and I spoke regularly of making a model train layout. We would sometimes go to Balboa Park, close to downtown San Diego, and visit the Model Railroad Museum, which still has several of the most impressive layouts in the country today. Then we would return home and climb into the attic of our house and talk about reengineering the studs of the roof frame in order to create the space necessary to build a huge track that would run above the living space in our house. At night, before I fell asleep, I would lie in my bed and stare up at the ceiling, imagining I could see through to the train unhurriedly winding its way around the attic.

My dad never pursued our model train layout. Like a lot of people, he talked more than he did. It is easy to get started thinking; it is hard to follow through doing. Eventually he sold the trains. I am not sure if he got bored or decided he needed the money. Perhaps he figured out that he wasn't the type to make a model train layout. (Now that I think about it, who *is* the type to make a model train layout?)

Years later, when I was out of the house, I started my own collection of Märklin model trains, the tiny Z-gauge kind. I remember setting up a short oval track one Christmas on a sheet of four-foot-by-two-foot plywood. My older daughters, eight and five at the time, and a ten-year-old boy from the neigh-borhood all gathered around and took turns moving the dial on the transformer to make the train go. My girls chugged the train along cautiously. The boy raced it around the corners, beg-ging it to fly off the track and break on the floor.

One night, I ran the model train when no one else was around. Only the Christmas tree lights were on in the house, and the nanoscale headlights of the tiny German train shone extra bright. I bent down so that the track was level with my face, and I squinted my eyes. The train was out of focus when it turned the far corner and inched toward me on the straight-away, moving along at a to-scale speed. The miniature engine grew clearer as it came toward my nose, which was resting very close to the track. Then the train turned across my face and out of my view.

I will be honest with you. I thought this would be the part of my book where I would tell you about the hardest thing for me to get rid of. Ridiculous as it sounds, I knew I was going to have to get rid of those trains when I started the 100 Thing Challenge, and it seemed to me that they would be impossibly hard to let go of. It was easier than I thought.

．　．　．

I really wished that my dad had made a train layout when I was younger. Probably more than I should have, I continued to wish for it when I became a teenager. And as I grew into a man, I still wished for it, even though I was no longer a boy and my dad could no longer build a model train layout with his Märklin trains, because he had sold them decades before.

Looking back on my life, I have wished a lot of things. No matter how much I have squinted my heart, whenever I reopen my eyes and things come back into focus, there is never a train layout.

Some things never get put together, or back together, in our lives. I have found that out. It is tempting to buy the materials we think we need to build what went unfinished in the past. American-style consumerism likes to sell construction stuff for that. Any one of us can go to the mall and browse through dozens of stores that will sell us all we need to fix things up. When we shop we sometimes act as if we are time-traveling general contractors. We buy components we think we'll use when we zip back to that dreadful moment in the past to patch things together. Make it all right. But the ruins in our lives don't get fixed. They get grieved for, or else they get messier.

We can put things right today but we need to refocus our attention. We can live the sort of lives that will get things working better tomorrow. But we cannot travel back through time and change the past. We don't change our imperfect lives by purchasing things right now that we think would have fixed our problems back then.

I think a lot of people do what I have often done myself. I have left a store with all the stuff I thought I needed to solve a problem. Not a real fixable problem, like the baseboard in our loft that is still not finished years after the project started. Instead, I try to take care of an unfixable problem, like my pretty good childhood that wasn't quite good enough—whatever "good enough" is. When I get home, I go to work. *Bang, bam, boom.* I start fixing. A little sweaty and out of breath, I stand back to regard my work, and here's what I see. There is that sadness I am trying to repair. The same darn grief. Only now there is a pile of consumer shit on top of it.

Do you know what that means? It means I now have to

shovel through new shit to get to my old shit. That's messy. And the truth is that the more I pile on top, the less likely I am going to be willing to dig.

Pretty soon, my past is petrified under layer after layer of detritus. If I'm not careful, I will be little more than an interesting archeological excavation for my great-great-grandchildren, if, out of some curiosity, they decide to bother to rummage through my past. A hundred years from now, they'll be tripping over boxes of antique model trains in this or some other attic.

"Look at this! Check out all these old German toy trains."

"Those belong in a museum."

"Why would he keep all this crap?"

"Well, I guess great-great-granddad didn't figure out that great-great-great-granddad was never going to build a model train layout."

"Poor fool."

＊　＊　＊

So I sold the trains. I listed my train collection on Craigslist. I waited three days to hear from the person who eventually bought them, even though I knew it took him only about three minutes to find the listing. If you've ever known a man who collects model trains, then you've known a man with obsessive-compulsive disorder. Men who go to model train shows and garage sales and browse eBay and Craigslist to purchase used model trains try to be coy. But it's good that they play with trains and don't play poker because they're as obvious as elephants. Years ago I sold a different train, not the Märklin trains, at a garage sale we had when we were living in Wheaton. Everything we were selling that day was laid out on our driveway and marked $.50 or $2 or $5. Everything except one battered-looking engine and a few cars in a tattered box, which I recall I had priced at $150. No one paid any attention to it, until the model train stalker arrived.

I had him in my sights the moment he showed up, and he had me in his. From the end of the driveway his eyes darted toward the train box, but he took his time browsing over to it.

"What are you getting for this toy train?" he asked, as if the scrap of masking tape didn't say exactly what I intended to get for it.

"Well, I don't know much about it," I lied. "It was a gift. But I think it's worth something, so I'm asking one fifty."

It was worth something. It was an antique Lionel train. By now the guy had probably soiled his pants, unable to believe his good fortune. You don't just happen upon a train at a garage sale like this one I had casually put out for sale. He wondered if it worked. I said I didn't know if it still ran, which was totally beside the point. He said he'd think about it and drove away. I moved the box a little farther toward the back of the driveway out of respect, and I determined to give him a deal when he returned. Of course he did.

My Z-gauge Märklin train collection went about the same way. The man who bought them held out longer. It took him and me about a month of pretending. I faked that I wasn't going to eventually sell him the trains for a price lower than I wanted to get for them. He faked that he had lost interest. But the deal got done and the trains were gone.

Now don't get me wrong. I like trains and think it's probably a good idea, even if you only have daughters like me, to keep at least one model train that you can inconveniently pull out every other December to put around the Christmas tree. I have nothing against model trains. But I sold them. And it didn't feel so bad. It actually felt really good. I no longer had to stress about building a train layout someday.

Have you ever actually seen a huge train layout? Can you even begin to fathom what kind of stick-to-it-iveness is required to make all those rolling hills and vast grassy plains with the millions of miniature blades of grass and little trees with minuscule maple leaves and all those tiny houses and the people who actually have faces? I am so glad that I no longer have to worry about doing that.

But my trains were not about the trains.

Letting go of the trains was inspirational and cathartic. I was also able to get rid of my rock climbing gear. I enjoyed rock climbing. That time I went to Joshua Tree National Park when I was in high school and climbed a couple of 150-foot routes was fabulous. The (maybe) four times I took my climbing shoes and chalk bag with me about an hour and a half's drive to Culp Valley in the high desert above Anza-Borrego Desert State Park to do some bouldering was great fun. The few times I went to the Solid Rock indoor climbing gym were a blast. But though I had some rock climbing gear and had even built that small indoor climbing wall at the back of our garage to use to stay in shape, I was never going to be a rock climber. None of that gear was ever going to go anywhere near a huge granite face in Yosemite. I had wished to be a rock climber. But I am not.

After purging my toy trains and rock climbing gear, it was so nice to no longer be burdened by what had gone unrealized in my past. I felt free to be the kind of guy who thinks model train layouts are cool but who would never actually take the time to build one. I was no longer oppressed by the knowledge that I owned track I hadn't put together and trains that weren't running. I felt free to be the kind of person who is impressed with rock climbers but who would never actually find himself attached to a rope, gripping a sliver of rock hundreds of feet in the air. I was free to appreciate these former interests of mine rather than worry about not participating in them.

The 100 Thing Challenge proved a handy way to get rid of stuff that was never going to fix my past or make me someone that I was not. It turned out I had quite a bit of stuff for that purpose. I had a lot of shoes, for example, shoes for all different kinds of manly purposes:

- Snow boots for men who live and work in rugged, wintery areas of the country. I owned them to keep my feet from freezing in case I ever traveled to a snowy region to split firewood or went back to Chicago.
- Cycling shoes for men who ride their bicycles a hundred miles or more a week, like I used to do years and years ago. I kept them, even after I had sold my bicycles, just in case I bought a new racing bicycle and again started riding hours each day.
- Outdoor soccer cleats for men who, well, play outdoor soccer. I had bought these cleats when I tried to play intramural outdoor soccer at Wheaton College with undergraduates even though I was a graduate student in my late twenties. I played only a few games and it nearly

killed me trying to keep up with the eighteen-year-olds. But I kept the cleats in case I started to age in reverse.

- Indoor soccer shoes for men who play indoor soccer. I had played quite a lot of indoor soccer over the years, though I had not played for several years before the 100 Thing Challenge started because I never did start aging in the other direction. Instead I went the way of all men who grow older. In that process I ripped up the meniscus in my right knee and had to have surgery. The surgery went just fine, but I determined it was best to pursue lower impact sports lest my left knee suffer the same fate.

Those four pairs of shoes were simply leftovers, I suppose. Some people are just plain pack rats and keep things like unused sporting shoes because they cannot bring themselves to throw the shoes away or donate them to charity. Despite my interest in stuff, I'm not a hoarder. I don't mind tossing things in the trash and I like to donate stuff to charity. I kept those snow boots because I wanted to split firewood. However, we live in winter-warm San Diego only a little way from the moderating effects of the ocean. In eight years we have never had morning frost on the ground or on the north slope of our roof. Moreover, the fireplace that came with our house has a switch that turns it on and we're not legally allowed to burn real wood in it because our house sits right beside hundreds of acres of natural kindling. In fact, we put the piano in front of the fireplace to hide it because

I think it's embarrassing to own a fireplace that turns on with the same *clickity-click-click* as the burners on our kitchen stove.

It felt really good to pack the snow boots, cycling shoes, and soccer footwear into a bag that I left at the Goodwill drop-off. In that same bag I put a pair of black dress shoes and two pairs of brown dress shoes that I would wear to work in order to look more professional than I actually am. I also shoved two pairs of slippers into the bag, even though I could not think of anything in my past I was trying to repair by owning slippers. They had been gifts, and I'm not a slipper-wearing kind of guy.

I filled up other bags. I filled them with dress shirts and the old anorak I wore when I would go skiing back in high school and college. I also sold things at garage sales. I sold some weights and a workout bench that I used some but not that often because I'd much rather work out by running or surfing or backpacking, even though I hardly have time to do those activities. That's why I sold the different topographical maps of the Sierra Nevada mountains I had hiked around before and will surely hike around again. But I knew I wouldn't be prioritizing backpacking during the year of my 100 Thing Challenge.

Eventually it got easier to let stuff go. It wasn't, I should point out, always easy to actually get rid of my things. The economic and social structures created by American-style consumerism make it a cinch to buy stuff but rather difficult to get rid of stuff, unless you're willing to make a mess of the world and throw stuff away. I regret that as I prepared for my 100 Thing Challenge, I did have to throw some perfectly good things away. Mostly though I sold or gave my stuff to others. Stuff like my:

1.   **golf clubs**
2.   **guitar**

3. balance board
4. yoga mat
5. backpack
6. Campagnolo Croce d'Aune rear
    derailleur
7. shoehorn
8. compass
9. magnesium fire starter stick
10. USB headset with built-in microphone
11. pewter Gollum
12. pewter Beorn
13. pewter hobbit (These three items
    were gifts. No, I do not play
    Dungeons and Dragons)
14. Harry Potter figurine
    (Nor Quidditch)
15. old MacBook G4
16. nose-hair trimmers (A "gift" from
    my wife)
17. Canon SLR camera
18. Canon 17-40mm lens
19. Canon flash
20. Gitzo tripod
21. camera bag
22. a lot more clothes
23. many odds and ends, pencils, pens,
    and knicknack junk

Purging stuff provided the momentum that I needed to get into a new habit of living, one in which I could resist new acquisitions for a year's time. As I got rid of many of my possessions I had to let go of some of the expectations I'd placed on my past. Thus, an unexpected consequence of downsizing to get ready for my 100 Thing Challenge was that the project became reoriented. I became less concerned about doing this crazy simple-living experiment in order to mend holes from my youth. The 100 Thing Challenge freed me up to more honestly explore hope for my future. It turned from a punitive project into an exercise in faith.

■ ■ ■

Despite my past, and in some ways because of it, I am living what many people would consider the American dream. But I've remained a restless wanderer in my soul. So, then, have I really arrived? Looking back on my time of purging for the 100 Thing Challenge, I now recognize that the very act of getting rid of all my stuff forced me to question the dream life that those things were supposed to occasion. And more than that, purging made me question what I had been trusting my life to and what I had been relying on to patch up the past in order to make a fantasy future. Religious guy though I was, had I truly been putting my faith in little plastic trains to fix some part of my youth and then turn me into someone I am not? Was I an idolater, or was I just an idiot?

Faith is not an option for humans. I like what Wendell Berry says about it: "Our instinct for faith is like a well-bred Border collie, who, lacking cattle or sheep, will herd children or chickens or cats. If we don't direct our faith toward God or into some authentic 'way' of the soul, then we direct it toward progress or science or weaponry or education or nature or human nature or

doctors or gurus or genetic engineers or computers or NASA."*
To his list, let me add, "or shopping."

We people simply must put our faith in something. But
what do we trust?

A lot of educated, thoughtful, well-meaning people will
spend hours and hundreds of dollars buying their rascally child
this year's must-have toy at Christmastime. A lot of overworked,
distracted, sort-of-nice husbands will purchase diamond ear-
rings to make things better with the wife they are ignoring.
Gadget purchased. Household calm. Jewelry bought. Wife satisfied. We put an impressive amount of faith in the capacity of
material things that other people make to repair the troubled
circumstances of our own creation.

You know the saying "What is the definition of insanity?
Doing the same thing over and over again and expecting different results"? Every time I bought some new thing for my trains,
I was looking for a different result. I was expecting that my
dad would have followed through. So here's something else to
consider. It's flat-out dumb to trust something we buy at a store
to undo what has already been proven a failure. I *am not* suggesting that my father is an overall failure just because he didn't
make a toy train layout in the attic. He simply failed to follow
through in that matter. (And as I have already said, I think it
was wise that he didn't.) But I wanted him to. And I felt a loss
of sorts because he didn't. And so in one remarkably trivial way,
I shopped for the same thing over and over again, imagining
different results.

What I have found about buying things and dealing with my
life is this: I often buy things as an act of foolish faith, which is

* Wendell Berry, "The Conservation of Nature and the Preservation of Humanity," in
Another Turn of the Crank (Washington, D.C.: Counterpoint, 1995), 76–78.

the same as wishful thinking. I am trusting that some*thing* will make some other thing better. I wish certain turns of events were not the case that already have been the case, and I want to buy a product to ensure that I get what I wanted *back then*. But the past is what it is, and no store on earth is going to settle my past accounts.

Real faith cannot be bought at a store. We cannot pay money for it. Faith is the means by which we take our incomplete and imperfect lives and do something marvelous with them. We cannot use a credit card or even cash for something so wonderful.

7. The Hardest Thing to Cut

Before I tell you about the experiences of actually living the 100 Thing Challenge and my reflections on those experiences, I need to confess what was the hardest thing for me to purge. I'm chagrined to share this part of my story, and especially embarrassed to admit how I came to own the last things I eventually gave up.

You could say that the hardest thing for me to give up was the idea of being a master artisan. But since being an artisan isn't a "thing," I'll confess that it was my woodworking tools, which I hoped would get me to the level of master artisan, that were hardest for me to part with.

Mostly I'm content with the frame God placed me into, but when I imagined myself a master artisan, this is how I envisioned it: I would be about 25 pounds heavier (180 pounds), about four inches taller (six feet), and my hands would be covered with calluses. Also, for some inexplicable reason, I would know how to skin several kinds of animals. My desire to be a skilled woodworker was more a dream to be some made-up, romanticized character than a real person. Because in real life I do not fit the profile of this imaginary craftsmanly hunter. Moreover, that kind of larger, harder, and more skilled man wouldn't have gotten his woodworking tools by selling a stuffed animal, which is how I got my favorite tool, my plunge router.

The stuffed animal in question was an unregistered Webkinz Cheeky Cat that my mom gave to me when I was thirty-six years old. If you don't have kids in the right demographic you will need to know that Webkinz are a toy craze that started a few years ago. The stuffed animals each come with a sealed tag that includes a unique code that a child (and, it turned out, a good many adults) can use to register the toy online. This registration process adds the animal to the virtual Webkinz world, where at the bidding of its owner, it is able to travel around, build a house, buy all sorts of consumer goods, and, just to make sure kids grow up ready for the real world, play Vegas-style gambling games to earn the Webkinz money they need to purchase all their virtual stuff.

Once the Webkinz craze took off, the company that made the stuffed animals recognized an opportunity. They could retire certain animals. If an animal was taken off the shelves at Hallmark, it would become more valuable because demand would exceed supply. That proved an opportunity for consumers. They simply needed to buy as many of these stuffed animals as possible, hoping to scoop up one that Webkinz would stop producing. If they did, they would be sitting on a mini-eBay fortune. My mother took this course of action with abandon, which is how she came to own a retired Cheeky Cat that she graciously gifted to me.

On the day I received the Cheeky Cat from my mom, I listed it for auction on eBay and immediately the bidding took off. Several people offered to buy it outright . . . for $100! I knew I was on to something, so I resisted the cash in hand and let the auction run its course. The cyber-gavel fell to close the auction and a woman, I think she was from Texas, won that Cheeky Cat for $325. *She bought a $15 stuffed animal from me for over three hundred dollars!*

I should have mourned that foolish woman. Instead, I used her money to buy one damn sweet router, an Australian-made Triton 2¼ horsepower plunge router that cost me only $200. Blinded to reality though I was, my master artisan plan seemed to be working. I felt brilliant.

I also purchased, from Rockler Woodworking and Hardware, a router table package that came with a free Porter-Cable router. A free router that, on account of my sweet new Triton, I did not need and so could sell on eBay for $100, which I duly did. By the time all the transactions were complete, I had taken one $14.98 stuffed animal plus about $100 of my own savings and turned it into a centerpiece of my fantasy woodworking shop worth $600.

(I should pause here to admit that this kind of scenario has happened before. I have pursued my consumer impulses to the financial injury of another soul. In that way my personal history has often mimicked the history of American-style consumerism, as I strive for a brighter future on the wounded backs of my accomplices. Aping the justification we hear from our shrewd culture of materialism, I say that it is the other person's fault and I am just taking advantage of the situation. True enough. But let's be honest when we speak of this kind of industriousness. The indefatigable man is disturbingly weak when the formula for success involves the undoing of someone else. In my rush to get to my dream, instead of balm and empathy, I have often gone at the wounded person with salt and a PayPal account.)

· · ·

For a while I had been reading Taunton Press's *Small Woodworking Shops*, a beautifully photographed and illustrated guide to setting up a shop in tight spaces. I made unostentatious sketches of our two-car garage. On paper, half the garage was devoted to the hobby I planned to nurture: furniture making. Or was it toy making? I had no interest in cabinets. Even before the 100 Thing Challenge, I had an aversion to the storing of too much stuff. Unlike my notions of the ideal artisan, the plans for my little shop were modest. I wanted to make a wooden chair and eventually a wooden rocking chair. There's this idea I've had for making a kid's fishing game with wooden fishing poles that have magnetic hooks and hand-carved fish that have a piece of metal inserted into their puckered fish lips.

But I couldn't help myself; I kept flipping to the chapter "Dream Shop in the Woods," by Les Cizek. The chapter toured the woodworking wonder-shop of Cizek and his business partner, Harry Van Ornum, who together run Four Sisters Woodworking in Fort Bragg, California. Their shop is a good deal bigger than half my garage. Four Sisters Woodworking is actually more than four times larger than my entire garage. And that's just their machine room, where they rough-cut lumber and finish it with a gorgeously macho thirty-six-inch band saw and a huge sliding table saw. They also have 720 square feet worth of workbench space, where they can finish their projects with hand tools, free from the dust and noise of machines.

Often I sat in my bathroom long after my business was done and looked at every detail of every picture of that shop. I said to myself, "I'll need to get more than a Triton plunge router."

And I did. A plunge router is a marvelous power tool. It can shave the edge of a board flat or cut decorative trim around the board's perimeter. It can cut a groove, called a dado, into a board, which can be used to support the edge of another board. Think of a bookshelf. A plunge router can "plunge" into a board, so that a dado can be cut, say, from the center of the board to one side, instead of across the entire face of the board. It's a handy tool that I was glad to own. And I had the router table, which was basically just a small workbench that held the router upside down, allowing me to use my hands to manipulate the wood I was cutting instead of having to hold the router itself. I had a compounding miter saw. I had a random orbit sander and a Dremel tool and a handheld circular saw.

When gathered together all of these tools hardly made a woodworking shop, but that was beside the point.

Over the years I bought unpowered hand tools, too. I bought a Japanese handsaw. Actually, the Japanese handsaw, which I dutifully purged for the 100 Thing Challenge, was a delightful tool to use, and I miss it. I already owned an old hand plane that belonged to my grandfather, and I bought another hand plane on eBay. Like the handsaw, the hand planes were a pleasure to operate. I had built a sharpening station that I used to make their blades of those hand planes phenomenally sharp. It gave me primal pleasure to shave a hair's width of wood with those hand planes. Also, I bought precision engineer's squares, which I needed to set up my router table for exact cuts. I bought lots of clamps for clamping pieces of wood together when I glued them. And I bought an antique bench vise that I scrubbed clean with mineral spirits. Then I bought the materials I needed to build a sturdy little workbench where I could mount the vise.

I think I was restrained in my tool purchasing, though perhaps I was on my way to excess. There were tools I did not buy that would be necessary if I ever was going to master woodworking. I didn't own a band saw or a table saw. I didn't own enough clamps, because you can never own enough clamps. I didn't own hand tools like chisels and a mallet. But my problem was still there. I did more than just get a bunch of woodworking tools and enjoy using some of them. I started imagining more of them and of myself. Somehow a picture, foggy at first but then after staring at it over and over again becoming more clear, developed in my mind.

The picture that came into focus was an image of me at some time in the future, standing in my woodworking shop. The shop in this scene wasn't situated in half a suburban garage. The shop was a separate building from the house. There were grassy fields around the structure and a gravel drive leading up to it. On the outer perimeter of the scene were large oak trees. The shop had a jointer. It had a band saw. It had a table saw. A large workbench with two vises. There was a whole wall of clamps. In that shop I saw myself lording my artisan skills over pieces of wood. I was master of the tools I would use to break the wood apart and reform it into whatever I chose to make.

For the sake of the 100 Thing Challenge, I put that fantasy up for sale.

The small workbench I had made of three sheets of glued hardwood ply, poplar trim, and a refurbished vise I sold to a guy who was coming back to woodworking after a time away. He told me he'd moved into the area and was setting up a small

shop and my sturdy little workbench would be perfect. When he
told me that he had moved to San Diego, he sounded like he had
left something uncomfortable wherever it was he came from.
He sounded like a person who was going to try to start over.

The router and router table I sold to a young man in the
military. He was a skilled woodworker, able to make cabinets
and furniture. He was taking advantage of the timing of my
deal, for I was selling my router and router table for less than
they were worth in order to get rid of them before November 12.
Yet he was not going to make use of the router and router table
for some time because he was deploying to Iraq by Christmas.
If he ever made use of those tools, I don't know.

I sold my compounding miter saw and a small collapsible
sawhorse to a middle-aged man. He found my tool listing on
Craigslist and looked up my address by using my cell phone
number. He also read my blog and knew about the 100 Thing
Challenge. I think he learned that I was a Christian by reading my posts and he revealed himself to be Jewish by wearing
a T-shirt that said something about the Holy Land when he
came to pick up the tools. I think, I'm not sure, he did that
just to let me know he had taken the time to find out a little
bit about me.

I cannot remember who bought the Japanese handsaw or
the old hand planes. I think most of the remaining tools—the
circular saw and the random orbit sander and the Dremel tool
and others—were sold at a garage sale. I forget the details.

Whatever the particulars, the tools eventually were gone. My
woodworking ambitions were put on hold. And in addition to
looking at living a year with only one hundred personal possessions, I was no longer pretending to be an artisan on the
weekends. I determined, too, I'd try to stop daydreaming about

being a master woodworker with a spiffy shop on several acres of land.

Why did I fantasize about becoming an artisan, a master woodworker? (I do think we pick these ideas on a whim.) Men have been known to fantasize about more interesting things than tools and wood. Some men would have thought about guns or fantasy football or race cars. Why would I zero in on the thought of being an accomplished woodworker? I cannot tell you for sure, though I do have some suspicions.

If you've ever made something out of wood, you know there's an almost teleological pleasure in the experience. A woodworker takes a tree—most likely it is considerably older than himself—and he cuts it up and turns it from a tree into, say, a bench for the porch of a house. A couple can sit beneath a living tree holding hands, chatting, laughing, and getting to know each other. Just the same, they can sit on a wooden bench on a porch. God makes trees, though. Whereas people make wooden benches. Whether or not I had silly ideas about being a master artisan, working with wood is a genuinely human act, and so I was in a way genuinely attracted to woodworking.

Not all people are, however, interested in tools and wood. I figure that in my case there was some nature and nurture involved in my attraction to this particular hobby. As I have mentioned, I like to use my hands. If writing, for example, didn't require me to tap-tap my fingers on a keyboard, I don't think it would be such an important part of my life. Sometimes when I sit down to write, I think about my hands and fingers as much as the story I want to tell. So I guess I was predisposed to a hobby like woodworking. Also, I was introduced to woodworking by my dad, who was not himself a marvelous woodworker but who made some good stuff with wood: a poker table, a doll-house for my sister, bookshelves for the study. He let me help as a young boy, and I'm sure that led to my appreciation of wood-working as an adult.

One more reason for wanting to be an artisan stands out: the desire to master a skill. In my life I have thought that if I could master one skill, then I would be somehow settled, con-tent. I didn't think that if I were to master woodworking I would be "done"—done being a husband, done being a dad, done being an entrepreneur, and so on. I don't really expect to be done until I'm dead. But for some reason the idea of mastering a craft promised for me a payoff—the notion of contentment. I would be settled in who I am. Rather than striving, I would have reached a destination, a place of rest and satisfaction. Like most people, I am relatively good at a lot of things but an expert at none. Maybe just the mystery of not knowing what mastery feels like was enough to make me fantasize about its beneficent effects on my life. Being a master is not unlike living a fantasy existence: both are slightly beyond the average person's reach. Or, at least, the kind of mastery I dreamed of was out of my reach.

As I thought about this in the weeks it took me to sell all my woodworking tools, it occurred to me that our human experience demonstrates that the correlation between mastery and contentment is suspect. Though we see lessons of failure and ruin in the lives of people who pursue mastery with self-ish insistence, we are ourselves apt to keep striving to master something, like a skill, or to achieve some idea, like the dream life, with the highest hopes for our sense of happiness. I wanted to be a master woodworker so that I could arrive at a place of contentment. Neither the skill of woodworking nor the sense of contentment I thought it would bring me was for sale. Tools were for sale, though. And so I bought tools.

After selling the tools and thinking about my time with them, I came to understand why mastery is not the road to a finish line of contentment. Mastery is a journey without final arrival. This is the response of the best "masters." For example, those people who, by their exceptional use of tools, we call master artisans are proud of the epithet but are themselves aware that they have reached no state of repose. The master confronts a problem in need of a solution, not through perfection, but by skill and creativeness. The belief that a master has arrived at an endpoint is antithetical to the very character of a master, whose contentment exists in the knowledge that she possesses the mind and physique to participate in her craft, not to dominate it. It needs to be added, the master's wisdom includes recognizing and accepting problems for which there are no good solutions and making compromises that cannot be described as superior. We call the person of skill who cannot accept limits pathological.

■ ■ ■

But there is a craft that is within our reach to master, or at least the skill we can come the closest to mastering: the craft of finding contentment in less than perfect circumstances. The craft of being, no matter how skilled and no matter how much stuff we own, an average human being whose life doesn't need to be domineering in order to be progressive. I had a lifetime's worth of stuff. Stuff that suggested that even if I thought contentment wasn't for sale, I wasn't ready to walk away from retailers to find satisfaction elsewhere. But now I had. Almost all of the personal belongings that I had ever owned were gone, even the hardest ones to let go, my woodworking tools. I owned less stuff than I ever imagined I would. And a new attitude was developing in my soul.

I was ready to begin the 100 Thing Challenge. I had gotten down to fewer than one hundred personal possessions. It was indeed hard to get rid of all that stuff, to sell it or give it away or simply toss it into the trash. It was *really* hard to get rid of some of that stuff. Most of all, it was tough to give up my hope of being someone I am not and not likely to become.

And that, like a good spring cleaning, was a refreshing way to prepare for the 100 Thing Challenge. Looking ahead to my year of living with few possessions, I felt like I had room now for something else.

Part Two

The Challenge
Takes Off

8. My 100 Thing Challenge Begins

It felt a long time in coming; in fact it was. From the time I dreamed up the 100 Thing Challenge in the summer of 2007 until I officially began on November 12, 2008, more than a year had passed. Some of that time quickly slipped by in distraction. Pressing life responsibilities like making money and raising children and procrastinating, among other duties, got more of my attention than I gave to preparing for the challenge. But in some stretches, the days moved slowly and with much difficulty. Paring down my belongings to one hundred personal items sometimes felt like pushing water uphill.

Also, in the year plus it took me to get ready for my 100 Thing Challenge, word got out about my project. From the time I first wrote about the idea online until the time I actually started living it in real life, the 100 Thing Challenge grew progressively more popular. It got to the point where if you typed "100 Thing

Challenge" as a search in Google, my blog was the first hit. If you typed simply "100 Things" then the *Time* magazine article that featured me was the first hit, and my blog was the second.

The physical demands of living life while preparing for the 100 Thing Challenge wore me down. And the newness of being a subject, albeit in the grand scheme of things a relatively minor subject, of media attention made the days leading up to the start of my 100 Thing Challenge emotionally laborious. I was tired and I was confused.

You'll have to forgive me, then, for what I wondered on the morning of the twelfth of November 2008. I wondered if my hour-long commute to work that day would be different. A little prideful and a little paranoid, I wondered if any of the drivers I passed on the freeway would think, "Well, look at that. There he goes, the 100 Thing Challenge guy." I wondered what work would feel like. Would anyone comment? Would the mundanity of office work become more vital now that I was living a certifiably different lifestyle? I wondered what arriving home would feel like. It was my birthday after all. Would my family throw me a party? Would it be a 100 Thing Challenge–themed surprise party? I don't much like surprise parties for myself and didn't really want one in honor of the 100 Thing Challenge. But maybe I kind of did.

Most of all, I wondered if the 100 Thing Challenge was going to be like a switch. November 11, 2008, the switch was off. November 12, 2008, the switch was on. Would it be the case that from that moment, and for the rest of my days on earth, my life would be different, and noticeably so?

Nope.

· · ·

I don't say this to dismiss the efficacy of the 100 Thing Challenge. It has proved remarkably beneficial, in ways I expected and in ways I could not have anticipated. Neither do I wish to cast doubt on the testimony of the thousands upon thousands of people who have taken the challenge and have experienced some kind of instant change or even epiphany in their lives. I am apt to believe the claims of people who have had turnaround moments, or at least I want to believe them. The day the 100 Thing Challenge started, however, I did not turn on my heels 180 degrees, forever forging a new life direction away from American-style consumerism.

In fact, on November 12 2008, my day was much like any other. Normally I wake up at five a.m. and leave the house before my family gets up so that I can beat the rush-hour traffic. This day was no different. I went to the office, I put in a day's work, and I came home. And like I usually do when I get home from work, I walked to the mailbox. There I collected, along with a couple of bills, a Patagonia catalog. The fact that I received a Patagonia catalog, filled with tempting adventure things, on the day I started my challenge was amusing to me. I was reminded that consumerism is a nuanced behavior that involves a measure of ambivalence for many people. Some companies, it seems to me, operate as if they are uncertain about American-style consumerism, too.

I have complex emotions about Patagonia. For many years I have had a love-hate relationship with the company. In some ways Patagonia is the antithesis of American-style consumerism. The "Footprint Chronicles" on their Web site, for example, brag about the company's efforts to be environmentally and socially responsible, but they also detail the ways in which the company fails in these areas. Patagonia at least attempts a level of transparency that isn't the norm among companies. It says it wants to do what's right and proves its intentions by detailing how it doesn't follow through. But in other ways, Patagonia appears to be one of the pinnacles of American-style consumerism—an ultimate brand. The Patagonia brand persona, the countercultural dropout who prioritizes demonstrable adventure over purchasable coolness, is the epitome of consumer irony. Patagonia has become the go-to brand for those who are unbranded.

. I cannot say that I'm reconciled to Patagonia's duplicity. I can say, however, that I've made peace with their products. The Patagonia products I own are among the highest quality things that I possess:

1. **R4 fleece jacket**
2. **Capilene 3 thermal shirt**
3. **Capilene 3 thermal pants**
4. **rain pants**
5. **wrinkle-free button-down shirt**

■ ■ ■

Patagonia is, in my eyes, a symbol of the intricacy of the American consumer's situation. As we shop, when do we transition from searching for the best-quality product to seeking the best-branded product? When is the moment we stop looking for something of value and start desiring something that we think will make us more valuable ourselves? These are not easy questions to answer. For anyone who likes outdoor adventures, they are particularly hard questions to tackle while flipping through a Patagonia catalog.

The catalog was a harbinger of sorts. A challenge to my challenge. A forewarning that just because I had decided to change, the world around me wasn't going to become different. Sure, some people are going to embrace consumerism with gusto. Others are going to reject it like a nun. But for most people, getting stuff is complex. Consumerism isn't something to turn on or turn off. Possessions: how we acquire them, why we acquire them, what meaning we assign to them—these are not simple issues. The 100 Thing Challenge wasn't going to be a simple project.

■ ● ■

That catalog came in the mail, but the birthday presents came from my family. I had some worry that someone would play a trick and deluge me with gifts. It would have been a funny prank, but my wife and children aren't tricksters. On the evening of my thirty-seventh birthday, they played along with my 100 Thing Challenge in considerate ways.

Leanne bought me new windshield wipers for my car. Since I count my whole car, a sixteen-year-old Mazda 929, as one thing and not all of its parts as separate things, this was a great gift that didn't count as a new thing. Moreover, she figured that she was saving my life by giving these replacement wipers to me, and she might have been right. We don't get much rain here in San Diego, which is all the more reason to have impeccable windshield wipers. When it does rain, drivers lose their carriage. There's no telling when they'll slow down or speed up or swerve or crash into you. No telling, that is, unless your windshield is as clear as possible.

I also knew that Leanne's gift was as thoughtful as it was precautionary. It was a gift with meaning. When she was growing up, her family never replaced the windshield wipers on their cars. So as a child she was driven around in the rain appalled and scared. When she gave me new windshield wipers for my birthday, I knew that she was doing more than giving me a gift that didn't break any 100 Thing Challenge rules. She was giving me a gift that was repudiating a bad habit from her family's past. This was encouraging to me. I was, after all, attempting to do the same thing. Her gift was an oracle: bad habits can be broken.

My daughters, too, were thoughtful. They gave me two vanilla bean pods. And here I must confess something to you that will likely make you think I am boring. I love vanilla. Not only do I love vanilla, I don't love pretty much any other sweet taste. Well, I do like chocolate. But I love vanilla. If given the choice of any flavor of ice cream, I'd choose vanilla every time. In fact, if given the choice of any flavor of ice cream except vanilla, I'll almost always go without a scoop unless I'm trying to be polite to the person who offered. One time my wife got some vanilla-scented lotion that she used to keep her skin soft, and I seriously thought I was going to bite her. I had to force myself to resist. My love for vanilla and my affection for her were almost too much for me when combined. Anyway, I sliced open one of the long pods my daughters gave me and crammed it into a bin of sugar that we used to sweeten our coffee. Within a day or two the sugar absorbed the vanilla flavor and our coffee was all the more delightful for months.

. . .

It took only a few days for the equivocal nature of consumerism to present me with a dilemma. I had not been paying much attention to the ramifications of all my purging, especially the downsizing of my wardrobe. The truth was that my day job didn't require me to dress up, so I could get away with the same business casual outfits week after week. Like my work attire, the climate around here doesn't change much either, so weather had not been on my mind when selecting what clothes to give away. Eventually my sparse selection of clothes was going to cause me trouble when winter came to San Diego. But a couple days after my 100 Thing Challenge started, I did realize that my lack of warm garments was going to be downright dangerous when the opportunity came for me to travel to Montana.

I had been invited to host a table at the Helena Education Foundation's "Great Conversations" benefits dinner and to present a talk at Carroll College about American-style consumerism and the 100 Thing Challenge. When the challenge started, my trip to Montana was only a week away. A quick check of the weather forecast and it dawned on me that I was going to freeze to death. Something needed to be done. Something needed to be bought.

My wife suggested that I go to The Gap and buy a wool sweater. I could wear it over a shirt and under a jacket to make my outfit toasty warm. This seemed like a good plan, and since I try to be a good husband, I took her advice and went to the mall. But I felt guilty and kept looking over my shoulder as I walked through the mall. It seemed like I was a criminal returning to the scene of my crime. Perhaps because of the self-awareness with which I entered the mall and walked to The Gap, I didn't notice much of anything else. I made my way quickly to the store and then to the shelf with the wool sweaters and then to the register and then back out to the car.

I was struck by an unfamiliar feeling. In the past I had shopped at the mall completely self-absorbed but hardly at all self-aware. Often I have gone to the mall fully concentrating on myself, unleashing my energies to find an outfit that would make me look cool or smart or mature. I've shopped in this state of mind without being aware of whether or not I actually am cool, smart, or mature. And I don't think this experience is unique to me. American-style consumerism promotes the action of shopping for ourselves without nurturing the attitude of knowing ourselves. In fact, the advertising and salesmanship at the mall seems geared toward assisting us to be ever more unaware of who we really are and always more concerned about who we are not.

When I went to get the sweater at The Gap, however, I wasn't very self-absorbed. Sure, I was thinking of myself. I was thinking that I wear a size medium. I was thinking that I don't like V-neck sweaters. But I wasn't lost in my thoughts about myself. Instead I was thinking pretty realistically. I went about my shopping aware of myself. I didn't think the sweater I bought was going to make me more cool, smart, or mature. It was going to keep me warm. I felt simply like I was just an average guy who thought he needed a sweater. And that's what I was. I was a guy who went to The Gap and bought a sweater he needed. I don't think that American-style consumerism wants us to think like this, to think realistically about ourselves.

That wool sweater did a moderately good job of keeping me warm in Montana. Helena was *cold*. It was so cold that the small commuter plane that took me there from Seattle shivered as it touched down on the runway. (And it bounced. And it rattled. That was one tiny plane.) As you might expect, once I was out of the plane and meeting my hosts and learning about the community, the sweater purchase and any thoughts about stuff faded into the background. My plan was to suffer through wearing a suit for my lecture at Carroll College. In fact, I learned that Montana has about the best dress policy in the entire United

States. My hosts, the college's president and his wife, suggested I just wear jeans and the wool sweater. "This is Montana," I was told. "No one cares if you're dressed up." Neither did I. So I took their advice.

The lecture about American-style consumerism at Carroll College went well, I hope. Unfortunately I had come down with a wretched cold and was losing my voice. But I managed to choke out my talk to a crowd of about 150 people and chat with a few of them afterward. Montanans are very hospitable and I felt comfortable enough up front to make some observations while I spoke. I stood behind the lectern reading my paper and intermittently thought:

- Many dozens of people of all ages, family histories, shapes, and sizes have congregated, some traveling miles in the freezing cold, to listen to a random California guy talk about consumerism. Human beings are utterly remarkable. Why do we give material possessions so much of our attention when we people are so much more fascinating?

- While it is true that Montanans don't much care about what I wear, they all sort of care about what they wear They all look the way I'd expect Montanans to look. Jeans, warm jackets, boots. Of course not every single one of them looks exactly Montanan. But the overall fashion of the crowd is not what I've seen in traveling to, say, New York.

It isn't what I'm used to in California. This reminds me that though material possessions can divide people, our stuff can also serve as common ground. Our personal things can become community bonds. That, it seems to me, is a good use of stuff.

- People actually care about how American-style consumerism is affecting their lives. All these people politely staring at me, smiling and nodding their heads to show me that they are listening, actually care about the struggles they feel at the mall. I'm up here jabbering away, not because I'm someone special or overly insightful, but because enough people in Montana feel the same pressures from consumerism as people in California, Florida, Colorado, and all the other states in this country, and even many other countries around the world. Consumerism is a big issue in all our lives.

The day after my talk at Carroll College, I had plenty of time to reflect on all of this. I completely lost my voice. Instead of visiting a few classes that morning and afternoon at the College, I sat on a couch drinking cup after cup of tea in silence, praying that my voice would return so that I could be conversational at

the Helena Education Foundation benefits dinner I was supposed to participate in that evening. Fortunately, my voice did
recover—barely. I met more kind and gracious Montanans. We
talked more about consumerism. We uncovered more of the
complexities of stuff, discussing how things can be both a detriment to our relationships and can also bring us together.

Traveling home from Montana, the gravity of the topic of
American-style consumerism settled on me. We're all in this
together. I mean, we humans are all in a lot of things together.
But some of our shared experiences are of greater concern to us.
Consumerism is one of those topics that we all directly experience, whether we have so much stuff that we feel weighed down
by our things or whether we have almost no things at all and
wish we had more. We're in this thing together. It's an important topic.

Consumerism is such an important topic that an average
guy living an average life in an average suburb can elicit the
attention of people the world over and get himself invited to
another state to talk about his experience. Not only that, it isn't
one of those boring topics. It's not one of those lectures you go
to and just sit in your seat and listen with the same amount of
enthusiasm as you show watching your fingernails grow. Consumerism is a topic that people feel they can engage with. They
have something to say. They have experiences to share. They
have stuff they want or don't want, things they purge or things
they have kept and for all sorts of reasons. It was important to
me to experience this level of interest for myself.

I think of myself as something of a techie guy. I know my
way around a Mac. I'm not fazed by Facebook. I've blogged for
a decade and I am comfortable embedding and adding nice-
looking bells and whistles to my Web site. Still, there was some-

thing inspiring about being able to give a lecture about the challenge so soon after it started. I didn't record a podcast or a webisode; I sat in a room and spoke to people face-to-face. I gave what would have at one time been called a talk. And then I sat next to people I didn't know at a dinner designed to celebrate conversation and talked with them about what I and they were doing.

What every one of us was doing that weekend was participating, actively engaging, in a discussion about consumerism. It felt good for me to see people react favorably to a point I made, to get the feedback and reinforcement, or, by the same token, to have someone disagree and make a different case. When you are seeking reactions, it's helpful sometimes to see it in their faces as well as hear it in their words. The level of interest people showed in the 100 Thing Challenge surprised me from the beginning. I regularly had to remind myself, "People really *are* intrigued by my challenge." Being with these Montanans discussing consumerism, I took this as an affirmation that the 100 Thing Challenge truly did have something to say to others.

THE 100 THING CHALLENGE LIST

On November 12, 2008, when I started my 100 Thing Challenge, this was my list of personal possessions. You'll note ninety-six things. This was never a precise science.

1. ESV Bible
2. NRSV Bible with prayer book
3. hand-me-down Bible
4. wedding ring
5. library
6. journal
7. mechanical pencil
8. ballpoint pen
9. wallet
10. sunglasses
11. watch
12. iMac
13. MacBook Pro
14. HP printer
15. external hard drive
16. microphone
17. cell phone
18. headphones
19. camera
20. SD card for camera
21. home office desk
22. home office chair
23. desk lamp
24. file cabinet
25. side table
26. car
27. *Planet Earth* DVD
28. toothbrush
29. razor
30. travel/work backpack
31. garment bag
32. suitcase
33. backpacking backpack
34. tent
35. sleeping bag
36. sleeping pad (lightweight egg-crate kind)
37. sleeping pad (self-inflating kind)
38. stove
39. cook set
40. spork
41. headlamp
42. pocket knife
43. rock climbing wall
44. climbing shoes
45. chalk bag
46. mittens

47.	wool hat	76.	jeans
48.	rain jacket	77.	jeans
49.	rain pants	78.	jeans
50.	thermal shirt	79.	button-down shirt (long-sleeve)
51.	thermal pants		
52.	wicking shirt	80.	button-down shirt (long-sleeve)
53.	wicking shirt		
54.	running shorts	81.	button-down shirt (long-sleeve)
55.	running shoes		
56.	canvas dresser for clothes	82.	button-down shirt
		83.	button-down shirt
57.	T-shirt	84.	button-down shirt
58.	T-shirt	85.	button-down shirt
59.	T-shirt	86.	button-down shirt
60.	T-shirt	87.	brown belt
61.	T-shirt	88.	brown shoes
62.	T-shirt	89.	sandals
63.	T-shirt	90.	underwear
64.	board shorts	91.	undershirts
65.	shorts	92.	socks
66.	PJ pants	93.	Moo.com personal business cards
67.	fleece jacket		
68.	suit jacket	94.	*Need* magazine subscription
69.	suit pants		
70.	tie	95.	*Backpacker* magazine subscription
71.	dress shirt		
72.	dress shirt	96.	award-winning self-portrait oil painting
73.	business casual pants		
74.	business casual pants		
75.	sweatshirt		

9. Imprecise Goods

I shopped on Black Friday. It feels important to get that confession out sooner rather than later in part two of my book. In the fall of 2008, during an unprecedented global recession, only two weeks after the 100 Thing Challenge officially began, on the day after Thanksgiving, when millions of economically ill-tuned Americans rushed to make purchases, I too bought something.

Shopping on Black Friday seems about as antithetical to the 100 Thing Challenge as could be imagined. Black Friday has come to epitomize American-style consumerism. Families, communities, whole regions put everything else in their lives on hold and focus all their energies on acquisition. The day is a day of getting. Things for ourselves. Things to give others. We buy things we have had our eyes on for most of the year. We buy things we just cannot pass up on this special day of exceptional sales. On Black Friday, I too gave in.

You probably expect better of me. Truth be told, I avoided the topic with friends and acquaintances for the next few days. I even dodged one person I know who practices simple living. On Monday after the holiday weekend, I spotted him just across the way at work and ducked in the other direction. I avoided him because I did not want to have to justify myself to him. I will not attempt to justify myself to you either.

Well, except to say that my wife and I were on a date. What's more, our kids were having a sleepover at their grandma's house. So we were on a date *and* feeling carefree. Plus, I truly needed a jacket suitable for work, yet functional enough for nonwork wear. It so happened that just such a jacket was on sale at REI, the store we stopped in to find a pair of brown Mary Janes for Leanne, who only had sandals at the time. And it was cold outside.

I like the new jacket well enough. Really, though, it is not as comfortable and it does not make me feel as dapper as the one it replaced—a ten-year-old faded wonder that I purged on the lead up to the 100 Thing Challenge. That old jacket was surely made by elves who, for a brief moment in textile-labor history, acquiesced to work for J.Crew. It was light and warm and fashionably cut. It was the color of the pale green ocean on an overcast day. Back then I had timed my purchase just right, when J.Crew still made magical clothing. (I have kept a J.Crew corduroy shirt from that same era. It is one of the most marvelous shirts I have ever owned.) Now though, the purchase of my new jacket was risky. If I got caught, I would have to do some fast talking, which, just to be clear, I could have done.

According to Rule Number Eight of the 100 Thing Challenge: "I could get new things. But I always had to remain under one hundred things total. And also if I 'replaced' something,

I had to get rid of the original item before I got the new one." These criteria were all met when I made my Black Friday purchase. The total number of personal possessions I had at the time was in the mid-nineties; thus, even after I was rung up at the register, I still owned fewer than one hundred things. The beloved old jacket I was replacing had already been dropped off at Goodwill, so I was not adding a redundant thing to my list. (In fact, I had given away quite a few jackets by then. A tweed sport coat from Joseph Abboud. A dark gray suit jacket from Nordstrom. A black vinyl-like jacket from Banana Republic. A brown fleece jacket from REI. A navy blue thick wool jacket from The Gap. An orange anorak from Eddie Bauer. A technical maroon waterproof jacket from Mountain Hardwear, which I gave to a friend at work. I ousted all of those jackets before I finally gave in and ditched my favorite one of all, the old J. Crew marvel.)

I should say too that, unlike so many purchases from my past, this one was done with real money, not a credit card. It was a sound acquisition, even by the abstemious statutes of the 100 Thing Challenge.

But does that make it right? My Black Friday purchase fit well within the boundaries of the 100 Thing Challenge rules. That is for sure. What feels less certain is whether or not I, the 100 Thing Challenge guy who turns his nose up at American-style consumerism, should have made a purchase on Black Friday, the advent of consumerism's holiday season.

The 100 Thing Challenge is not about precision.

This will come as a disappointment to some. After all, "100" sounds pretty exact. You might say that if I am going to take a stand then stand tall. If I am going to encourage others to follow, then do not get sidetracked. As long as I am going to begin a worldwide anticonsumerism movement and write a book about it, for heaven's sake, I ought to have exactly one hundred things and live like a freaking troglodyte who never steps foot into a store for a year.

It's just that life and little life projects like the 100 Thing Challenge are not so tidy. Tidy would be not buying anything at all for a year. So I wasn't tidy. And if I wasn't striving for tidy then Black Friday was as good, or as bad, a day on which to make a purchase as any other. Tidy would also have required that I own exactly one hundred things for my 100 Thing Challenge. Tidy would have put the 100 Thing Challenge completely in order. I picture our lives the way that the novelist Frederick Buechner describes a fairy tale: "It is a world where goodness is pitted against evil, love against hate, order against chaos, in a great struggle where often it is hard to be sure who belongs to which side because appearances are endlessly deceptive."* Living precisely does not guarantee results, because it is hard to be sure that we are always doing precisely the right thing.

American-style consumerism shines with an illusion of precision. But we are human beings. For us perfection is a false impression in the way that there really are no Barbie-perfect models with glossy skin and ideal proportions whose pictures sell all the products we buy. Even the ones who come close to ideal after a lifetime of exercise and surgery are airbrushed to perfection once the photos are taken. They are just right, just not real.

And real life is not precise, no matter how much we shop— *or don't.* The insistence that we can and should get things just right at the mall confounds reality. I do not want to suggest that

---

* Frederick Buechner, *Telling the Truth* (San Francisco: HarperSanFrancisco, 1977), 81.

American-style consumerism is the only context in which we pursue a version of the good life that is, in fact, not obtainable in our earthly lives. Before industrialization and the rise of mass consumerism, there were other utopian schemes. In this day and age, we try to buy perfection. But perfection is not for sale.

With my challenge and its rules and parameters, I ran the risk of having one starry-eyed plot replace another. To replace my quest for the American dream with my 100 Thing Challenge was not the point. It would not do to substitute days we "have to shop" with days we "must not shop."

There are positive feelings we get by replacing consumerism with nonindulgence. The way in which we approach material possessions is not the same as the way we choose what flavor candies we like and dislike. There are real virtue-building aspects of simplicity. And if we had to choose only one lifestyle that we had to live consistently, I'd endorse a lifestyle of simplicity. By the world's standards, or at least by the standards of the United States and other Western economies, I can say that I do live a life of simplicity. But our lives are too complex for following one set of rules. Our lives are more nuanced than will fit into this or that pattern all the time.

. . .

I think that I was doing exactly what a mature human should have done when I bought that jacket on Black Friday. I was being responsible, joyful, and imprecise. The purchase was economically reasonable and it did not break any rules I had set down for the 100 Thing Challenge and announced to the world on my blog. And I bought it on a great date with my wife. I felt cozy and warm when we left REI. We drove to the beach town of Del Mar and had dinner at Il Fornio, a scrumptious Italian restaurant. By the time our food arrived, it had started to rain lightly. We were sitting under the covered patio, but the cover was drafty and a little leaky. I was glad to have the jacket.

Do you know how wind and water are unstoppable? The smallest cracks give wind and water all they need to creep through and make it chilly and wet. Well, I am also kind of drafty and leaky. I cannot stop up my fissures with purchases at the mall. Neither can I hold back the wind and the water with my expectations of living a spartan life. If the 100 Thing Challenge were precise, it would eventually be blown apart. It would buckle under the torrential pressures of life. It wouldn't do me any good, and it wouldn't be of genuine help to other people who also live under the pressures of real life. If the 100 Thing Challenge were precise, at most it would be an entertainment in the genre of dark humor. It would be amusing to see me fail because that's all I'd be able to do if the goal were exactness.

That would make good TV, to watch the 100 Thing Challenge guy fall to pieces just before the episode ends. Next week it would be someone else. Eventually the whole cast would fly off the island and the show would end.

.   .   .

When I came up with the 100 Thing Challenge, I wrestled with how to make it real. I did not want the 100 Thing Challenge to be this season's whimsy. How do you make something real that could easily seem to others like just one more exhibition in the midst of our overstimulated society? After quite a bit of thought and prayer and conversation with friends and strangers about the details of the 100 Thing Challenge, I decided it needed to be imperfect. It could not be insulated from wind, rain, and the human world of foible. It could not be edited, the parts that

seem too honest, boring, or scripted sliced out in order to keep
my audience's attention.

"Huh? He's keeping 'one' library."

"That's lame. He probably sleeps in a hotel at night and goes
to his house only when they're filming."

"Oh, look at this. Now he's buying a jacket on Black Friday."

"*Whatever!*"

"Give me the remote. This 100 Thing Challenge is dumb."

Some people will call me a cheater. In fact, some people
have cried foul and told me that I am not really living the 100
Thing Challenge because of the exceptions I've made: the one
library; counting my underwear and undershirts and socks as
three "categories" of things; shopping for new things . . . on
Black Friday; still wanting more stuff. One poster on my blog
said anti-consumerism was neo-Marxist and a lively discussion
ensued about political philosophy. This is curious, since the 100
Thing Challenge is just a personal project I dreamed up one
random summer day in the long sweep of human history. The
way some people talk about it, you'd think that the 100 Thing
Challenge were an undiscovered attribute of the cosmos. As if it
were a law. Some people have criticized the irregularities of the
100 Thing Challenge as if the one inalienable rule of simplicity
is perfection. As if the simple life is the life without exceptions.

Of course, you know by now that I do not agree with such
evaluations of the 100 Thing Challenge or of life. These assess-
ments come from a culture of precision that creates bondage,
because there is no freedom when we are held captive to the
requirement of perfection. It's the way of American-style consumerism, which demands that we strive always for perfection.
Anything short of "exactly right" is short of the dream life. But
rejecting American-style consumerism with the same level of

commitment to exactness will only get us stuck somewhere else. Being an "exactly right" nonconsumer isn't going to work either. The perfect nonconsumer will fall apart just the same as the perfect shopper. Both are living lives in the service of onlookers who demand that other people do what they themselves cannot do. For some reason, these bystanders get a kick out of other people's failures.

There is, I believe, an abundance of good to be had in this world, and it isn't mostly found at the mall. As messed up as our world is—and the world is awfully messed up—there are endless opportunities to pursue good in our lives. But the way of the good life is ironic. It's unanticipated and unclear. The sun rises on evil and on good, it shines down on those who demand everything be perfect and those who recognize their own limitations and who show patience toward others. The real good life we pursue is filled with imprecise goods, things and actions that are not ideal but that will make our lives and the lives of others better.

A CHALLENGE CHRISTMAS

I started my challenge in November. From early November on, it's hard to escape the onrush of Christmas as retailers remind us of the true new meaning of the holiday season. I had an initial concern about my own Christmas, that I'd receive gifts I'd have to deal with in a spirit incommensurate with good manners: I would have to unload them as quickly as possible. I thought that enough people, certainly members of my family, were aware of the challenge and would refrain from giving, but in case I got anything from a couple of generous individuals, I performed a mini-purge of a few things.

I was more worried that I'd be caught up in stuff-longing. As Christmas approached. I caught myself thinking about the odd thing or two a couple of times but nothing really tempted me. The avalanche of catalogs and e-mail advertisements were not alluring and I was very happy about that.

It wasn't any new item I wanted but I did miss two things I had purged for the challenge. I'd replaced my digital SLR camera and its multiple accessories with a single point-and-shoot camera, but the new device just wasn't up to it. I like taking good-quality pictures and enjoyed sharing them with friends and family. This was a loss I felt heavily. And others told me they missed my nice camera, too. Sometimes a thing provides a way for people to connect. Cameras can be like that as long as you make sure you're not missing the event you're helping to record

I would have liked to have kept my laptop, an old Apple PowerBook, and to have retained the ability to write outside my home, but owning a laptop wasn't a pressing need in the middle of the challenge. When time came to write the book, I thought it might be a different matter. For the time being I'd do what I could at the desk. I decided I was happy with my state of mind: missing only two things badly and not coveting anything else very seriously. I was excited about my prospects for my Challenge Christmas.

Then Leanne jumped the gun. Nine days before Christmas, she bought me a pair of pants. They were nothing to do with Christmas and Leanne claimed I didn't have to address the pants under the terms of the challenge until I officially took possession of them. But the pants put me in a quandary. Rule Number Seven stated: "Once I received a gift, I had seven days to figure out what to do with it before it counted toward my 100 Thing Challenge." But the rules also said, "If I 'replaced' something, I had to get rid of the original item before I got the new one."

I had been thinking how amazing Leanne had been. She was parenting like a best-selling marriage and family therapist and cooking like a Pixar rat. Moreover, she was tolerant of me despite my occasional tired and grumpy moods. I was starting to think she was perfect. Then the pants. In fact, Leanne was trying to save me from myself. One day I went to work wearing my grayish suede pants and an orange plaid button-down shirt with my light brown slip-on shoes. I looked like a thirty-seven-year-old Frank Sinatra groupie. She was worried about me. Unfortunately her eye for men's fashion didn't match mine. She got me khakis from Costco. Khakis! I cannot stand khakis. But I took her hint. Even as I made her return the khakis, I bought a pair of brown cords.

In the end, I came out of Christmas with four new things, plus replacement underwear and undershirts. Two of the gifts I got rid of quickly (more about that tale later) and one I gave to my wife.

- **One fleece jacket, a Patagonia R4 (for all you brand-conscious readers), which is kind of bulky for fall hiking** and backpacking, but I traded the bulk for the coziness. It kept me toasty while sledding in the eighteen-degree weather the day after Christmas.

- Two sports jackets (about which, more later).
- One recycled material Starbucks mug. With my blessing, Leanne took the mug. I kept the gift card that came with it. Really, I could not have kept and made use of this gift anyway. My old Mazda, believe it or not, does not have drink holders. I'd have had to rest this tall, skinny travel mug between my legs for my commute. Not something I wanted to risk day in and day out.

10. Naturally, Our Stuff Goes Only So Far

T he way some boys want to grow up and play football in the NFL, I wanted to be an adventurer. There was no way it was going to happen. And yet, improbability has not stopped me from dreaming and even getting outside for an awe-inspiring hike every so often.

This adventure impulse confronted me over my challenge year because I kept a relatively large number of things related to the outdoors while laboring through the 100 Thing Challenge. Ten of my personal possessions were pretty much exclusively camping gear.

1. Osprey Atmos 35 backpack
2. REI half dome tent
3. Marmot Helium sleeping bag
4. Term-a-Rest sleeping pad

5.   **MSR Pocket Rocket stove**
6.   **MSR cook set**
7.   **Light My Fire spork**
8.   **Platypus water bladder**
9.   **Petzel headlamp**
10.   **Benchmade Mini-Griptilian pocket knife**

Sure, I often slipped my Benchmade knife into the front right pocket of my jeans and it came in handy while I was out and about. A few times I used my butane stove and cook set to boil water for tea in our living room, playing pretend adventure games with my daughters. In fact, that was how I almost lit the house on fire once. Yet those ten things listed above were really meant for adventures in the wild outside. As were the seven articles of sporty clothing I kept:

1.   **REI mittens**
2.   **wool hat**
3.   **Patagonia fleece jacket**
4.   **Marmot rain jacket**
5.   **Patagonia rain pants**
6.   **Patagonia thermal shirt**
7.   **Patagonia thermal pants**

Granted, these clothing items were less specifically adventure gear than my fifteen-degree sleeping bag. But I purchased them all, at one time or another, with adventure on my mind. I wore the fleece jacket quite a bit during the winter. Of course, pretty much any jacket would work here in Southern California to get me from a building to my car in February. I should just admit that the new Patagonia R4 jacket I'd received for Christmas appealed to me because, while it was cozy and warm in my hometown, it also would come in handy at base camp below Mount McKinley in Denali National Park in Alaska.

By now, the adventure-weighted makeup of my 100 Thing Challenge list did not end with my camping gear and sporty clothes. I'd taken up surfing. Thirty-seven years after being born and raised in Southern California without ever having touched a surfboard, I decided to paddle into waves for the first time. Surfing seemed adventurous, especially for me, because I have some fear of being drowned by a double-overhead wave crushing my head into a reef. I now had six things related to surfing (seven if you counted the rack on the roof of my car that I carried the gear on).

1. **Channel Islands 6' 9" Machado single fin surfboard**
2. **Xcel full wetsuit**
3. **O'Neill wetsuit jacket**
4. **Patagonia board shorts**
5. **plastic storage bin to hold my wet wetsuits in the car trunk**
6. **plastic water jug for washing salty ocean water off after surfing**

That makes twenty-three (or twenty-four) of my hundred things that were almost exclusively set aside for strenuous outdoor activities. I also kept one DVD, *Planet Earth*, which I use for inspiration to not be lazy and to actually get off my bed and get outside. But I didn't watch it very much during my challenge.

In the year of my 100 Thing Challenge, the closest those things came to an adventure of the sort I dream about was in January, when I used most of them to hike Rabbit Peak in the Santa Rosae Range near the Anza-Borrego Desert. There are no taller mountains farther south in California. At 6,640 feet, many experienced peak baggers claim it is a more difficult climb than Mount Whitney, the continental United States' largest mountain. Having summited Mount Whitney post-challenge, I can attest that the climb up Rabbit Peak is a comparable butt kicker.

I climbed Rabbit Peak with my buddy Marcus and one of his friends. We chose to hike it as an overnighter, making our way up to the lesser Villager Peak, where we spent the night. In the darkness of the next morning we brewed some coffee and then dragged our chilly legs onto the trail. The hike is twenty-two miles round trip. By the time I stumbled back down the last switchback of the desert-hard rock to make my way to the car in the late-evening sun, I looked like a savage and felt like shredded construction paper. It truly had been an adventure.

It was only one, though. The only major adventure of my 100 Thing Challenge year. Yet one quarter of all the personal possessions I "could not do without" for a year are adventure things. It seems like there's something going on in my closet.

. . .

I have tried to track down the source of my love for nature and desire for adventure. I've rummaged through memories trying to find the moment when I really noticed the earth, when the beauty and magnitude of forests and oceans and deserts and mountains first overwhelmed me.

My family used to go camping and fishing in the Sierras every summer. We would drive up California's Highway 395 to Bishop and camp at a campground. Then we would go to a lake and fish for trout.

In my mind's eye I can see the road winding up to Lake Sabrina, the parking lot, the boat launch, the path that crosses the dam over to our favorite trout fishing hole tucked in between large boulders. When you are walking over the dam and look down, there are always big fat trout staring up at you. Taunting. Unwilling to bite. One time I dangled a treble hook full of Velveeta cheese over the guard rail. I bobbed it up and down to make it appear enticing. I even whacked a huge brown trout right on his snout. Nothing. It did not even swim away. Trout are not easily embarrassed, and they aren't dumb.

Anyway, I do not remember the road or the parking lot or the dam on this one particular trip, which makes me think that it was not Lake Sabrina. What I do recall was that we pulled up to the campground in the late afternoon in a light drizzle. We half set up and then skedaddled to fish as the day turned to dusk. Whatever lake it was that we rushed off to, we fished on the flat side. Way across the lake was the real Sierras side. The Sierra Nevada mountains rise fast, leaping through the sky above the tree line, like chiseled multitudes jumping their way into heaven. On the barren face of the mountains across the lake where we fished, I saw lightning strike. I am sure I caught a trout that day. I always caught a lot of trout. But I don't remember it. What I remember was the lightning on the mountains.

It would have been possible, I think, for me to drop my pole right then and there and just go. To walk the dozens of miles and thousands of feet to the mountain where the lightning struck, and to stand forever soaking the scene in.

That might have been the moment something clicked inside me and I really began to love nature and adventure. It's certainly the most vivid of my earliest memories of the immensity of the natural world. It's the first memory in which I comprehended the lure of nature and the necessity of adventure. Forests, oceans, deserts, mountains. People. I think that is what is so appealing about the earth. How much we are like it. Teeming with life. Vast and empty. Polluted and on the brink of catastrophe. It's all familiar territory for us.

It must have been over twenty-five years ago. My father and I have not fished for trout in at least twenty years. My family never updated our camping gear. About the time that fifty-pound canvas tents went out of style, we stopped going to the Sierras. Of course, that means I have not watched my father grow old behind a rod and line, which is how many sons watch their fathers age. Though it's not the point of this story, there is something to be said for owning a fishing pole and using it. Fishing poles and tackle are as good an argument against the 100 Thing Challenge as any I know.

. . .

A few years back I met an attractive single woman when I was adventuring alone in the southwestern-most corner of Sequoia National Park. It takes about six hours to drive from my home to Mineral King, a rustic old mining town tucked at the base of the Great Western Divide. I had left on a Friday around three a.m. in order to get there early enough to do some hiking. Cold Springs campground in Mineral King was going to be my base camp for several day hikes into the mountains. None of my buddies could make the trip.

All the way up I was listening to weather band radio in my

old Subaru Outback, which has since fallen apart. Every few minutes the severe weather warning announcement repeated. The first big storm of the season was on its way, and it was pretty much aiming directly for Mineral King.

My rickety old wagon made it up the impossibly winding twenty-five-mile road from Three Rivers to Mineral King without incident. I pulled into lonely, quiet Cold Springs campground to find a beautiful lone woman loading one of the more well-appointed packs of adventure gear I had ever seen.

The truth is that I am a pretty shy and awkward guy. Just as some people wouldn't really know what to do with a microphone on a stage, I have always felt unsure speaking to women. Also, I am a Christian man who has been classically conditioned to bolt like Joseph fleeing from Potiphar's wife any time there is even a whiff of infidelity in the air. When I told my Christian friend Marcus (the same guy I hiked Rabbit Peak with) about the woman some time later, his brow furrowed and he quizzed me, "You know who that woman was, don't you?"

"No."

"Satan."

Holy crap! I hadn't thought about it like that at the time.

Actually, I don't think he had much of a point. First of all, it feels embarrassingly presumptuous for me to think this stranger had any intentions. And second, Satan is crafty and smart. The woman I met, whose name I never learned and who seemed like a very nice person, wasn't the sharpest camper on the mountain.

I was avoiding eye contact, just to play it safe. But she strolled by eating an orange and struck up a conversation while I finished pitching my two-person REI half-dome tent. Turns out she lived in San Diego, too. None of her friends could join her, either. And she was looking for sympathy. She was a manager of an adventure gear store and had left it in the care of a few employees who would probably screw everything up.

"Don't worry about it. They can handle the store for a couple of days," I encouraged. "Just enjoy your time. Where are you going?"

She had a mighty fine brand-name backpack. It just looked stuffed full of waterproof and 800-fill goose-down fabrics. She had coiled rope neatly dangling from one side and carabiners clipped on loops on the backpack. There was a sporty bandana holding her hair back.

"Hockett Meadow."

"Oh. I've never been, but people have told me it's beautiful." That's true. The first time I visited Mineral King and hiked to Monarch Lakes, I met some locals who said that Hockett Meadow is really pretty. And another time when I took my family a couple miles short of Cold Springs campground to stay in a cabin at Silver City Resort, the owners said that Hockett Meadow was a beautiful hike.

I looked at all of her topnotch gear. "You know that there's a storm advisory, right?"

"It can't be that bad. It's just snow."

I cannot recall if my eyes narrowed as I sized her up. What kind of smart-aleck chime was that?

"I don't have a map," she added.

She really said that. I double-checked: "You don't have a map?"

"No. How hard can it be to find Hockett Meadow?"

I wish my buddy Marcus had been there. The woman was clearly dangerous.

Later, after she trotted off on the trail to Hockett Meadow, I ran into a ranger. He asked if I had seen the woman who was out here by herself. I said to him that I had talked to her and, with my face crinkled contemptuously, I told him that she didn't have a map with her. "You might want to prepare for a rescue."

"It happens all the time."

People needing to be rescued all the time. I could think of no reason to doubt him.

"Are you the guy who's coming up here from San Diego by yourself?" the ranger asked.

"Uh, yeah."

"Your wife called and wanted to make sure you made it safely. She said to keep an eye on you."

And I cannot remember how I responded to that.

. . .

The first day in Mineral King I hiked around a bit. Back then I still had my nice Canon camera, which I later purged for the 100 Thing Challenge. (In the late summer of 2008 I listed it on Craigslist, and a young Brazilian man bought it from me. When he showed up to buy it, he was $100 short. I already had priced it low, so I held out He went out to get $20 from his mother, who was waiting for him in the car. She was going to drive him to the airport because he was flying to Brazil, where he was going to visit family but also photograph a wedding. So I sold my camera to him for $80 less than I wanted to.) To be honest, I regret having gotten rid of my camera. There is a connection between the world and the photographer. The pictures I took brought my photographic subjects and other people and me together. I think our best possessions, if we use them well, function that way. They provide us an opportunity to connect with the world and with other people.

I hiked about a thousand feet up the Timber Gap trail and looked back down on the glaciated Mineral King Valley. Have you ever stood alone and looked down a thousand feet into a valley several miles long and thousands of feet deep sliced into the earth hundreds of millions of years ago by a glacier? If you have your wits about you, it will make you want to cry or else whisper praise to God. What I have found, though, is that I oftentimes do not have all my faculties about me. Sometimes I do not think clearly enough to take in the beauty of the natural world that I claim to love so much. Sometimes at moments like that one overlooking Mineral King Valley I think, "Oh Lord God in heaven, if only I had a full-frame digital SLR and a wide-angle lens!"

That's one of the reasons that twenty-five percent of the personal belongings I owned during the year of my 100 Thing Challenge were things for adventuring. I dream of climbing mountains and spelunking and motoring a steel-hulled trawler around the world. I want to wander off and take it all in forever. I want to be on the edge of the mountain, ready to catch lightning. It seems like you need the right things to do stuff like that. So I get the right adventure things. But I end up stuck in camp, like that lone woman.

After returning from the Timber Gap trail, I spied her setting up her tent at Cold Springs campground. (The ranger later told me she had run into snow a few miles up the Hockett Meadow trail and decided to turn around.) I don't know much about people, so I don't really know for sure what kind of look she gave me. I looked down a half-dozen campsites and caught her eyes. If I had to say, I think it was a look of sheepishness. Or, it might have been loneliness, which for us humans is pretty much the same thing. Embarrassment and solidarity go hand in hand. Anyway, I saw her across the way that last time just before the sun went down and I headed over to my neighbor's fire to warm myself, drink cheap wine, and chat.

. . .

There is some truth in the fact that we need stuff to enjoy nature. I have a buddy who once drove through a remote part of the country when he was a newlywed. He claims—and thankfully there is no way to verify—that he and his young bride pulled the car over, stripped down to the buff, and went for a nudie nature hike.

The rest of us need to buy at least some stuff to enjoy nature. There actually are basic needs that adventure stuff meets. Survival needs, for example. When the weather dips below freezing, we need stuff. A jacket. Long underwear. A warm sleeping bag. When the desert floor is scorching, we need stuff. Shoes. A hat. A bottle to hold water.

My own opinion is that there is another, more honest reason we must carry stuff with us into the natural world. It is much the same reason that Adam and Eve covered themselves with fig leaves that were insufficient and God had to kill and skin an animal to make adventure gear for them. He had to do that because they could not make it out there in the wild as they were. And they couldn't fix things up on their own. Here is a reasonable truth we should come to grips with, which the 100 Thing Challenge has not debunked: we cannot get that far in life without adventure gear.

The crazy thing about most of us humans is that we cannot even get that far with adventure gear. We gear up and head into the natural world intending to hike right on through the pressures of work or the difficulty of a bad relationship, and lo and behold, a little bit of snow turns us around. No wonder we have such a hard time improving our career prospects and mending our relationships and other challenges like that. We cannot even make it a few miles up a trail wearing the finest adventure gear that money can buy.

Perhaps that is because we are not only hiking into the wilderness when we venture into the natural world. When we adventure, more than in almost any other activity, we are trudging, step by step, closer to ourselves. If we actually made it all the way up the trail, past the snow, over the mountain, we would come toe-to-toe not only with a beautiful meadow but also with our souls.

A year before my solo trip to Mineral King our family hiked in a huge meadow with some friends. We were all camping in the redwoods in Kings Canyon National Park. The meadow was created by the felling of giant redwoods a hundred years ago. We plodded over gargantuan stumps and through thickets and across river inlets. It was so incredibly wonderful. But I got caked in mud and itchy from wild grasses. One of our daughters tripped and tumbled down a stump, skinning her leg. Another one of the kids got pricked by a stinging nettle.

You know, meadows are really pretty in pictures. It's also a genuine pleasure to hike through them. But most meadows aren't as pristine as Julie Andrews's meadow in the Austrian Alps. Most meadows are beautiful *and* nasty. Like most of us.

Adventuring in the natural world requires that we explore ourselves. That prospect is enough to turn most of us around, or keep us at adventure stores shopping for protection. And shopping for protection isn't such a bad thing. We need it. As always, though, American-style consumerism entices us to shop for more than we need. It tempts us with adventure things meant not for protection but for perfection. If we gear up with all the right stuff, we will be brave. We will be physically capable. We will be expert navigators. We will not be insecure about how well we are doing at our job or whether or not we'll ever find a life companion. We will make it all the way to the top and look all around and be entirely content with the magnificent scene, and ourselves.

If American-style consumerism had its way, we would be beautiful and not nasty, which of course isn't natural. Which is another way of saying that if American-style consumerism had its way, we wouldn't be human. And that isn't much of an adventure.

A WINTER UPDATE

Periodically over the course of the challenge, I would do an inventory and check how much stuff I had. Stuff came and went. A few days after the challenge started, I got rid of the oil painting I made of myself that had won a first prize at the Del Mar Fair in 1990. My parents wanted to have it if I didn't, so I gave it to them. I don't believe I ever actually had exactly one hundred things and that remained the upper limit as I often hovered in the nineties. At the end of January I sold my sleeping bag and self-inflating sleeping pad. (A sleeping bag without a sleeping pad is little use, and not just for comfort—most of the heat we lose in tents escapes via the ground.) It was a very nice forty-degree down bag, but most of my trips would be more comfortable with a twenty-degree bag. I didn't have any trips planned that would require a bag, at least not for a few months, but I wanted to eventually replace the item. That brought me down to ninety-three things.

A few days later, on February 1, I checked and found that I'd bought five things since the start of the challenge and received two things as gifts that I had kept. At the same time, I had purged several things since the challenge started. I decided that I would take the whole month of February off—I wasn't going to buy anything for myself. I made that decision a little easier by, on January 30, buying myself a new laptop.

I'd purged my old laptop and felt the loss. Still, I'd resolved not to buy a new one. This is how I justified my decision on my blog:

> In my life I've found a simple rule to
> be worth following most of the time:

listen to your wife when she gives you advice and is not in a state of emotional upheaval. (Actually, it's not a bad idea to listen to her advice even when she is in a state of emotional upheaval, since you're probably responsible for the upheaval and taking her advice will likely fix everything.) Over some pillow talk last night my wife explained to me that a laptop would be really helpful for me to actually write this book I'm writing. And she said she'd love to send me away to some writing privacy several nights a week. And then she explained that she will be kind of embarrassed if I don't manage to get this book written. That last worry, of course, could lead to some major emotional upheaval. So I bought a laptop and plan to add several evening hours a week to my morning hours of writing.

. . .

Three months into the challenge, before I went to church one Sunday, I looked over the list to see if there was anything I hadn't used at all over the course of that quarter-year. At that point, I had ninety-three things and it turned out I had not used only two of them:

- the hand-me-down Bible
- one tie

There was one other item I wasn't sure whether to count as used or not: the suitcase. But we'd stored Christmas gifts from Santa in it, so I figured that qualified as use. So of my ninety-three personal possessions, I had not used only two in three months. That's not a lot of excess baggage.

I must have had too much time on my hands that day because I also figured out that most days I had fourteen things with me no matter where I was:

1.	underwear	8.	wedding ring
2.	undershirt	9.	watch
3.	shoes	10.	wallet
4.	socks	10.	journal
5.	shirt	12.	pencil
6.	pants	13.	sunglasses
7.	belt	14.	cell phone

. . .

So two percent of my personal possessions I hadn't used and fourteen percent I used every day. I'd shown myself that I could live with fewer than one hundred personal possessions. This quick count of my daily usage of things was a new eye-opener: it only took fourteen things to get through most days. Neither of those percentages is perhaps of note in itself, but if you look at the numbers a different way I think they're interesting. I used ninety-eight percent of my personal possessions every three months at the very least. Anyone can try a simple two-minute challenge—look in a closet in your house or apartment and check off the number of things that are yours that you haven't used in at least a year. Then determine if what you find out is notable. Without even looking, I'd predict that the potential for decluttering is significant.

11. Reactions to the Spectacle

Be cautious when you go out on a limb, and don't expect much assistance. I have learned that advice anew during the year of my 100 Thing Challenge. The reactions to my project from friends, family, and complete strangers reinforced it.

There is a frustrating element to the vulnerable feelings that accompany human risk taking. Consider, by comparison, what happens when a cat goes out on a limb. Everyone loves it! Kids shout, "Daddy, look at that cat climbing the tree!" Dogs race to the tree's trunk, their muzzles lifted upward in awe, barking out adulation. And if the celebrity cat were to get stuck? A concerned woman would call the fire department, and handsome firemen would race to the scene with hook and ladder to rescue the feline.

But climb a tree as an adult human being and passersby are likely going to call the police (or the asylum warden) to lock you up. No one is going to laugh or clap. Kids are going to cling to their parent's leg and nervously ask, "Mommy, why is that man up in the tree?" And can you even imagine what would happen if you got stuck? The jeers. The embarrassment. By the time you got down, you'd just want to crawl into a cave and disappear. But before you could find a hole one of your friends would be sure to find you and point out, "You shouldn't have been climbing that tree in the first place."

The world is full of advice givers. Quite a few advice givers reacted to my 100 Thing Challenge. Dealing with their advice was like a whole other challenge.

In the end I found that the advice givers were helpful in many ways. They brought clarity to the 100 Thing Challenge. There was something for me to learn from them, ways for me to grow as a result of their reactions to my project. Take my buddy Andy, an author I reached out to in the winter of 2008 after I landed a book deal to write about my experience. I was dealing with no small emotion, trying to process the media interest in the 100 Thing Challenge and the expectation that I'd write a wildly funny and insightful book about it. So I wanted to ask someone who had been through the process before, a successful author who had dealt with the pressures. I gave Andy a call. With all the comfort of an arm around a shoulder, my advice-giving friend told me, "Let's face it, the 100 Thing Challenge is a gimmick." Then, like a pat on the back or a friendly nudge under my chin, he added, "By the time your book is published, no one is going to remember what the 100 Thing Challenge was." Nothing like a boost of confidence for an anxious first-time author.

But a quality of all reactions is that they prompt reflection. At least I have found that I cannot rest until I've processed the advice someone gives me. I force myself to mull it over. I make myself calm down after I get mad. I insist that I ask myself, "Is it true?" So I considered Andy's reaction to the 100 Thing Challenge. He is a friend, after all, and I respect him quite a bit. People devise gimmicks to attract attention, either to themselves or to some concern of theirs. Was it true? Yes, I guess I do sort of like being talked about. There was something kind of appealing about having my name printed and the 100 Thing Challenge featured in the German *Financial Times*, Italy's *La Repubblica*, the *Washington Post*, the London *Times*, the *Guardian*, *USA Today*, and *Time* magazine. A reporter told me that Leonardo DiCaprio's agent told him that DiCaprio liked the 100 Thing Challenge, news that I pretty much liked hearing. There was a part of me that enjoyed the fact that *The Oprah Winfrey Show* called to inquire about my being on an episode, then called back another time to solicit my advice about their Earth Day episode. There seemed to be an element of truth in my friend's reaction. I was liking the attention. But how much?

Originally I approached the 100 Thing Challenge as a way to clean out the physical space around me in an effort to make more emotional and spiritual space inside. It was a personal risk. From the outset doubt has haunted me. I worried that, my stuff stripped away, I would uncover troubling facts not just about my excessive consumer behavior, but also about my anemic soul. That's not the sort of gimmick that an average person wants to draw attention to.

Not only that, but I found that among my family, friends, and acquaintances, the 100 Thing Challenge was beginning to define me. And I wasn't sure I liked that kind of attention. People reacted differently to the Dave doing the 100 Thing Challenge than to the Dave they had known before. Take my sweet wife. When I said to her, "I think I've lost my blue mechanical pencil," Leanne would not under normal circumstances have replied, "So you mean you only have ninety-seven things?" I received mild ribbings from colleagues at work. When I walked into a meeting to present a new Web site plan to the Point Loma Nazarene University cabinet, the president inquired if the piece of paper I was holding with my talking points was one of my things. (It wasn't. Technically the university owned the paper.)

If I had to identify the most common personal reaction to the challenge, it was that people were less sympathetic in quotidian situations, such as when I misplaced my pencil or when I carried a piece of printer paper. When my life became refracted through the prism of the challenge, empathy turned to curiosity. Another example: when I admitted casually I'd really like a new-to-me Subaru Outback wagon, I heard, "Oooh, so what are you going to purge to make room on your hundred-thing list?" No one said, "Yeah, I'm tired of my run-down car, too" or "Me, I'd love to get a Volvo." The 100 Thing Challenge came to outline the relationship boundaries with people who knew me. The normal social boundaries moved a bit closer. Sympathy was easier for people to get around.

This was all okay. I knew I had brought my changed status on myself. It's a condition of risk taking, this going out on a limb. You are exposed a little, and other people necessarily look at you in a different light. They wonder what this out-of-the-ordinary behavior says about you, about them, about everyone. I spent most of the 100 Thing Challenge period either at home or at work, but I often felt as though I were in a laboratory. Sometimes I was the one wearing the white coat and taking notes; on other occasions I had the fur and was locked in a cage running around and around on a little wheel. But if this was an experiment and I was the subject, I'd volunteered to be the lab rat.

Fortunately, it turned out that the arbiters of mass cultural gimmickry rejected the 100 Thing Challenge as an experiment to point cameras at. The 100 Thing Challenge was no mere contrivance, teed up for a publicity home run. The theme of the episode that prompted the first call from *Oprah* was "eccentric lifestyles." I had a genuinely delightful conversation with a producer. But in the end, we agreed that there wasn't much eccentric about the 100 Thing Challenge. My commute to work, my suburban house, my mutt dog and calico cat, my one cup of coffee in the morning and one cup in the afternoon—basically, my workaday 100-Thing-Challenge lifestyle didn't fit the formula of eccentricity that shows well on television. That was the same reaction of the producer from ABC's *World News with Charles Gibson*, who inquired about doing a "Day in the Life of the 100 Thing Challenge." He too felt like my life wouldn't make good TV. I don't think he could imagine a compelling lead, ("Watch next week as we visit with a guy named Dave who often wears the same shirt for two days in a row!")

My life didn't change enough to make the 100 Thing Challenge interesting, or interesting enough for TV. Or was that the interesting thing about the 100 Thing Challenge? Was it noteworthy because it is so outlandish for a middle-class American man to live with fewer than one hundred personal possessions? Or was it striking because, despite living with so few things, my day-to-day life didn't really change much? The answers to these questions are the naughty secret of the 100 Thing Challenge. Life is just about the same without an abundance of stuff—*shhshh,* quiet now—except without all that crap, there's more room for living life to the fullest.

But if I was determined the 100 Thing Challenge would not be purely a gimmick, it nevertheless outlasted Andy's other reaction. It never faded away. When Lisa McLaughlin wrote about it in *Time* magazine, she described the 100 Thing Challenge as a "grassroots movement in which otherwise seemingly normal folks are pledging to whittle down their possessions to a mere 100 items."* A grassroots *movement?* Something that had started as a harebrained idea in my garage had become officially described as a "movement." When she interviewed me in early June 2008, she told me that she and other people were talking about the 100 Thing Challenge over drinks and meals. I was skeptical. Over time, however, I heard this same story again and again.

Talking with a producer in the United Kingdom before a radio interview, he told me that his office had been discussing the 100 Thing Challenge for weeks. Well, actually, they had been arguing about it, the women making the case that it would be much easier for men to do the challenge than it would be for women. (I'm not a woman and so cannot say for sure, but I bet those women were right.) A *USA Today* article written in July 2009 that mentioned the 100 Thing Challenge featured the Crossing Church in Elk River, Minnesota, pastored by Eric Dykstra, who exhorted his congregation to take the challenge. Well into 2010, requests for interviews continued to come my way, and that despite my publisher's insistence that we tone down the publicity until the book was published. People remained interested in the 100 Thing Challenge. And interested people have interesting reactions.

. . .

* Lisa McLaughlin, "How to Live with Just 100 Things," *Time*, June 5, 2008.

The reactions, comments, and criticisms of other people were a humbling aspect of the 100 Thing Challenge. People who commented on my blog told me where they thought I was going wrong and where they thought I was doing pretty good. Kaya wrote that she agreed with the spirit of the challenge, but she herself kept an uncluttered home and valued many of her things, such as mementos of her family and art supplies. She wondered at the wisdom of my getting rid of things like my woodworking tools that I'd only have to spend money to replace if and when I ever changed my mind. Kaya spoke from experience, having moved abroad twice and returned home, each time purging and expensively rebuying her stuff.

On the other hand, Joe wrote of how he had turned up at college (at Point Loma Nazarene University, where I worked) a few years before as an undergraduate with everything he owned packed in the back of his Explorer. It wasn't as if the car was crammed full; he could carry all his stuff in one trip from the Explorer to his room. Joe wrote of how his possessions had "ballooned" in the interim, so he'd now need a U-Haul to move. He said that my blog was encouraging him to revert to a simpler way of living because possessions were getting in the way of what was important to him.

I understood what Kaya, and others like her, were saying— that some of the activities we value the most and that bring us pleasure, such as crafting, do involve the ownership of a certain amount of stuff. I also appreciated the criticism I received from people who didn't like all of my rules, or the exceptions I made to my rules, particularly the "one library" of books and the fact that I was sharing things like the dining room table, silverware, and kitchen sink with my wife and kids, who were not actively participating in the challenge. In the straitened economic circumstances in which we find ourselves, borrowing something from a neighbor rather than buying it for yourself makes good sense and I allowed myself that variance as well. I also wrote into the rules the ability to buy myself something new over the course of the challenge, as long as a few guidelines were adhered to, which meant I could look forward to upgrading my surfboard at some point in the future. Presenting the challenge openly and for what it was invited criticism and helped me as I explained (or justified) myself, enabling me to narrow my focus on why the challenge was important to me.

The fact that I did not count my shared bed among my personal possessions didn't diminish the lessons I was learning from the challenge, even if it seemed questionable to a couple of people. Someone named Lawsy commented on the 100 Thing Challenge page on my blog that the public wanted more commitment and drama than I was providing. "If you're planning a book based on this experience it's going to have to be more visceral than this. The public want to read about suffering and hardship and a man sticking solidly to his idea! They want to hear how your kids got rickets and your wife nearly divorced you because you forbade her to buy toilet paper." Lawsy declared the comment was "half-joking." And I think he's right. It's probably why I got only halfway to *Oprah* and ABC's *World News Tonight*. The 100 Thing Challenge didn't have a full portion of blood and guts.

. . .

The community that developed around the 100 Thing Challenge has grown into a kind of extended family to me. Some have been like siblings, like Teresa, who is a remarkable example of simplicity herself as she sails her boat around the oceans.

And like Adam, whose family, his young children included, went giftless for Christmas and happily focused on giving to impoverished people who have almost nothing. Some were like a wise and encouraging uncle, like "Somebody" who lives in Finland and helped keep me thinking and uplifted throughout the 100 Thing Challenge.

But I do have an actual extended family, not just Leanne, Lucy, Phoebe, and Bridget. I have parents and in-laws. My parents were born in the United States, but most everyone before them came directly from Italy. Once, when Leanne and I had been married for only a year and we were finishing up college in Chicago, we visited the small Italian church in Itasca, Illinois, that ancestors on my father's side helped found in the early twentieth century. After the service we spent about an hour greeting a century's worth of relative. Every encounter went something like this:

"David, meet Aunty Rosemary. Rose, this is Franky's son."

"*Ah*, Ruthie, he looks just like his grandfather Frank." (My dad is Frank Jr.)

"Rosemary is your great-uncle Gerry's (as in Giuseppe) cousin. Her daughter was married to Jim, your father's second cousin."

"Here, David, come here. This is Uncle Mike. Mike, this is Franky's son."

And so it went.

In addition to complicated lineage, Italian families are characterized by what I call "the big three." They are known for yelling at one another, eating with one another, and buying one another things. Now, it is true that all families argue, eat, and buy. But, one could say, Italians are like everyone else, only more so.

Everyone has conflict. Italians take conflict to new deci-
bel levels. Everyone enjoys a meal together. Italians eat a meal
together until they are stuffed senseless. Everyone likes to buy
and receive gifts. But the things Italians desire to get and give
are luxury things. Armani things. Prada things. Gucci things.
Ferrari things. Any *thing* that, even if it doesn't hail from the
homeland, smacks of swank.

You can imagine that Ursula, my mother, didn't take well to
the 100 Thing Challenge.

"What? So I cannot buy you anything?"

"Yeah. Just for a year."

"That's foolishness!"

"Foolish or not, *don't get me anything!*"

(Silent thinking and meat tortellini cooking.)

"So why can't I buy you an iPhone?"

"Mother!"

"Let me get this straight. If I buy you an iPhone, it replaces
your cell phone, right? I give you the iPhone, you throw away
the cell phone. Done. You see, it's not an extra thing. What's
wrong with that?"

And, of course, there would have been nothing wrong
with that. Except, for a lifetime—for nearly forty years—fancy
consumer goods had been central to my relationship with my
mother. Other boys' mothers made them study hard so they
would grow up to be lawyers. Other boys' mothers made them
play football so they would grow up to be athletes. At least once
a month my mother wrote a note with a fake excuse and picked
me up from junior high early so we could go to the mall for
lunch and to shop at Macy's. In high school, after our family
progressed comfortably into the middle class, our routine
changed: we started shopping at Nordstrom.

For the most part, our trips to the mall didn't change the way in which I operated in my youth, which was pretty much like any other guy. I played a rough-and-tumble sport—not football, but lacrosse. I owned a high-powered pellet rifle, which I used, though I now regret it, to murder birds around the neighborhood. And since I was already a screw-off at school, I wasn't destined to be a lawyer.

My mom's reaction to the 100 Thing Challenge—her frustration that she could not buy me more stuff—reminded me that the 100 Thing Challenge wasn't my burden alone. She loved me despite stuff, I'm sure of that. But material gift giving was important to her and to her relationship with me. Perhaps because my mom grew up in New York City in the projects, she appreciates material possessions in a way that I, having been given a comfortable life by my parents, cannot understand. This is not justification for excess. I am simply saying that I had to step back and try to sympathize with people who weren't as suspicious of material things as I was.

I have a sympathetic audience among the followers of the 100 Thing Challenge. We all feel comfortable rejecting fancy things that we don't need. It's harder, though, to justify rejecting a luxury gift from a person who really loves you and loves to show you love by giving you nice things. We simplicity-minded people think that a luxury item is frivolous. But what about the *gift* of a luxury item?

I resisted letting my mother buy me an iPhone. Instead I encouraged her to get me that Patagonia R4 jacket for Christmas in 2008, which she did. And I sensed she enjoyed buying it for me. Overall, my mother was a trouper. She mostly let me do my 100 Thing Challenge and held her tongue about it. She even talked about doing the 100 Thing Challenge herself, which would have been absolutely incredible to watch. I think she should, and should write a book about it. She has *a lot* of stuff, and she's a hysterical storyteller.

When we go out on a limb, assuming it's a big sturdy oak tree, if everyone climbed the tree with us then there wouldn't be much danger. We'd all be up there together. Yet that isn't what normally happens. We leave people down below gaping up at us. If we fall or the branch breaks, we're going to come tumbling down on top of them. The risks we take are not only our own.

I could not modify my consumer behavior without impacting others. My mom was one reminder of that. Just like buying isn't a solitary activity, simplicity isn't a lonely activity either. We're in it together. Other family members reminded me of that, too.

My sister Antonina was a frequent source of encouragement. She enthusiastically supported the challenge from day one, regularly commenting on my blog, e-mailing with suggestions, and musing how she might do some purging of her own.

My in-laws, Billy and Cathy, went along with the 100 Thing Challenge, too. To the best of my knowledge they never pulled Leanne aside and asked her why she married such a nut, though I did hear that they asked her a few times what the hell I was doing. Cathy figured it out and kindly bought me a restaurant gift card, a nonthing, for my birthday. Somehow, though, the 100 Thing Challenge never got fully explained to Billy, who got me four sports coats for Christmas. It caused quite a commotion and no shortage of laughter when he brought them out of his room where he had been keeping them while the girls opened their gifts. He told me he had found a great deal at Mervyns, which was going out of business. He lamented that when he went to try on one of the coats (Billy's about one and a half times bigger than me), he learned that they were not going to fit him.

"I'll tell you what. Let's just say that I keep these coats here, at my house. Then, if you ever need one, you just come over and borrow it. What do you say?"

Speechless, I futilely searched my wife's eyes for help.

"Well, uh, thanks. Wow, I will have, uh, a look at these coats."

Out of awkward politeness, I took two of the sports coats home. That week I quietly donated them to charity and all of us didn't talk openly about them anymore.

My dad, on the other hand, understood the 100 Thing Challenge right away. Initially I think he reacted with mild indifference to it. He likes luxury things, so he might have been skeptical. But my dad has not always had much and has worked remarkably hard for what he does have now. He's progressed from running his own yard-trimming business after returning from Vietnam to being a very successful technology manager and eventually a business owner. He has a discerning eye for business. And he has a skeptical eye. One day about halfway through my 100 Thing Challenge my dad brought up one of the most common suspicious reactions to the project.

"Hey, Dave, I've figured something out."

"Okay. What is it?"

"Well, if everyone did your 100 Thing Challenge, no one would buy things anymore and you would be responsible for destroying the world's economy."

Responding to that reaction deserves a chapter of its own.

A NEW FRUGALITY

The day-to-day life of the challenge was not without its excitement. In April, Leanne bought me a new pair of pajama pants because my old ones had holes in them. The old ones went in the trash, so this was a replacement transaction. Around the same time I bought some books on consumerism (which I might have borrowed to avoid the ironic twinge), but books are part of my library.

The truth was, I was coping well at not buying stuff. I even resisted a couple novels I would normally have bought even though it wouldn't have added to my official total of things. I started spending less time on the Internet. I read the blogs I was interested in and the news, but retailers' sites didn't do it for me anymore. Challenge-style living crept into other areas of our life. One night in April, the kids slept over at their grandma's. Whereas, on another occasion, we might have lived it up in a hotel and had an expensive dinner, Leanne and I stayed home and ate in. We were consuming less and we really felt the result financially—we were in much better shape than we'd been in in years.

That's not to say that I didn't still need new things, or, perhaps more accurately, want them. I wanted a new pair of hiking or running shoes. With a couple of friends I had made a promise that we'd undertake nine adventures in 2009 and by the end of April we'd done only one. My middle-age spread was coming on early. I needed those shoes. When REI sent me a twenty-percent off coupon, they made the decision a little easier for me. Speaking of footwear, I also developed a yen for a new pair of work shoes. I had a pair of all-purpose brown shoes that were starting to show their age.

I also wanted to subscribe to U2.com, which would cost $50

a year but which would allow me to listen to all their music. I was planning to see U2 at the Rose Bowl later in 2009 and I wanted to be able to refresh my memory of the lyrics. I believe that music isn't something we can really "own." Before recorded music, we had to pay someone to play our favorite song for us and now we demand the right to own the thing forever? But subscribing to a Web site isn't a thing, even less so than a download from iTunes, so my dithering didn't affect challenge tallies either way.

Aside from these items and a few clothes (shirts and jeans), there wasn't really anything else I wanted. There was one instance where I almost fell victim to temptation and bought something I didn't need. I ran out of .7mm pencil lead and went to the store to buy a refill—which they didn't have. I prefer thicker leads, and I saw that they had 1mm leads and 1mm pencils. So I nearly bought a new mechanical pencil! If I'd kept having weak moments of covetousness like this, I don't know how I could possibly have made it to the end.

I did buy and count a microphone at the end of April for Leanne and I to start podcasting. Leanne's a big podcast listener, and we had been talking about starting one ourselves, "Schooled in Marriage," about the ups and downs of married life. The microphone put me, as far as things were concerned, at ninety-seven.

Then, just like that, I was at the halfway point in the challenge. Leanne and I visited the mall and I realized that I hadn't been there in six months. I had put some distance between the mall and me, and I wasn't missing it. At the time I said, "If you stay away from something for six months and then go back and you realize you don't need it anymore, it's not just not necessary; it wasn't a good thing in the first place." I felt the mall, the place where American-style consumerism is perhaps strongest, wasn't needed and it wasn't missed. Thus was the challenge changing my life, very subtly but significantly.

After I blogged about going to the mall, I received a perceptive and amusing comment on my blog from Leanne. "I totally agree with you, honey," she wrote. "But if we hadn't gone to the mall, we would have missed that marvel to behold: the man walking his huge, black potbelly pig on a leash. Come on, that was worth it!"

12. The Short Answer to the Big Question

When I spoke with people about the 100 Thing Challenge, they asked me all sorts of questions. Do my kids count as things? (Yes, kindergarten teachers, there is such a thing as a bad question.) What about underwear? These questions were broadly all the same: Is that shirt collar, shoe lace, pant zipper, or swatch of pocket lint one of your hundred things? After that, inevitably someone inquiring about the 100 Thing Challenge would ask the second question that always came up. This was the big one. Wouldn't the 100 Thing Challenge destroy the world economy if everyone did it?

Of course, this gave me a powerful sensation of cosmic proportions. It felt similar to the rush of adrenaline I got when my friend Sue from Nashville said she heard that I was the person who had started Facebook. The world contains another person who actually believed me capable of starting Facebook!

(She must have missed how I thought up YouTube, too.) I felt shaky realizing that hundreds, maybe thousands, maybe tens of thousands, of people wondered if the 100 Thing Challenge, which I devised, was capable of ruining the world economy. It was like having "the button" in front of me and my finger poised to press it.

If I were ever to be put in that position, obviously there's no way I'd ever, ever, ever push the button. There's no such button among my possessions. Seriously, I don't want the 100 Thing Challenge to ruin the economy of the world. But the potential damage that could be wrought if everyone lived a life of simplicity is a valid question, I suppose. I feel compelled to offer an answer. I am not, though, an economist or futurist or policy strategist who might be able to answer this question with authority backed by years of research. So I will have to address it briefly and with a good amount of humility. Yet I am bold enough to say that I think I have a perspective that is valuable. My view gave me the bravery to do the 100 Thing Challenge and not back away from it once people started taking notice. I'll defend the challenge and what it represents as valid and useful. And so I ask that you give this short chapter consideration as you think about your personal consumer behavior and the larger economy that is dependent on your spending habits.

Before jumping into the hypothetical ramifications to the economy if "everyone" were to do the 100 Thing Challenge, let me reiterate what I hope I've already made clear. The 100 Thing Challenge isn't for everyone to do. I've already suggested that the 100 Thing Challenge isn't a good fit for kids—my daughters showed me that. But I also do not think it's a smart choice for some other people. U.S. senators have lots of fancy suits and all sorts of mementos they've collected throughout their years of public service. I'm just shooting from the hip here, but if I were to suggest, for example, a project for a U.S. senator, I'd propose the "100 Lobbyist Challenge." The senator would allow only one hundred lobbyists to wine and dine him during his term. I suspect that would do more to combat the senator's self-importance and temptation for unethical behavior, and it would likely enhance federal legislation in a way that benefited American citizens and the rest of the world. Youth, politicians, rock stars, junkyard operators, and probably a dozen other categories of people are not good fits for the 100 Thing Challenge.

Joe, a respondent on my blog, pointed something out to me when he said he'd carried all his worldly goods to college in the back of a Ford Explorer, with plenty of room to spare. When we're students, or anytime we're getting our feet under us after we've left home, we're often not the most acquisitive of people. Single people in their twenties are often more likely to spend money on having a good time, whatever that means to them, than on a lot of stuff. I'm not saying many young people aren't interested in stuff—of course they are. The reason advertisers target younger people is because they have some propensity to blow their money on less-than-vital purchases. But often, before they settle down, they're moving, from home to college, from college to a town for a job, or from a town without any jobs to one that might have some, possibly. So perhaps people who've lived in only one place for three years for the first time since they left home, or some other definition of "settled," should think about the challenge. They've stopped being rolling stones and might have started to gather some moss. It's to be hoped they have a little more money than they did, perhaps some to spare at the end of the month. Then this kind of lifestyle becomes a conscious choice, which is what it has to be for it to have any punch.

But for argument's sake, let's ask the question: Wouldn't it destroy the economy if *everyone* did the 100 Thing Challenge? I believe the short answer to that question is "Maybe, but almost certainly not." If, for example, everyone did the 100 Thing Challenge and used their newfound freedom from material possessions to drop out of school or quit work, forage for beer and pizza, and have sex with each other, well then, yes, it would eventually destroy the economy. But of course not everyone taking the 100 Thing Challenge would do that. If everyone did the 100 Thing Challenge, some of them would surely use their newfound freedom from the bondage of American-style consumerism for more profitable endeavors. I'd estimate that there is an extremely low probability of everyone doing the 100 Thing Challenge and also becoming an economic and social deadbeat. So maybe it would destroy the economy if everyone did the 100 Thing Challenge, but almost certainly it wouldn't.

This short answer needs to be qualified by a medium-size principle that will clarify the economic philosophy behind the 100 Thing Challenge. It's the guiding economic concept of the 100 Thing Challenge and a foundation for my critique of American-style consumerism. Here it is: whenever we use our money and talents well, it is always good for an economy.

I say that it is good for "an" economy because it is good for multiple economies, not just "the" economy. The word "economy" derives from the Greek words *oikos* (house) and *nemein* (manage). A sound economy is literally a "well-managed household." When we use our finances, individual skills, and community resources adeptly, we benefit not only our own households but also our neighborhoods and country. When we use our financial resources poorly and squander our individual skills and passively ignore community responsibility, then we all suffer. There's enough blame to go around. The subprime mortgage disaster that contributed to plunging the U.S. economy into recession required the complicity of overeager homeowners, unethical lenders, gutless regulators, and entitled politicians. The recession, however, affected everyone. Basically, we're all in this thing called "the economy" together.

This is perhaps the most important point for me to make in this chapter. It's simply a misnomer that our individual consumer choices are *our* choices. There's a tremendous irony in the pervasive notion of individual consumer choice. The belief is that we are free to make choices for ourselves. We think that, claim that, and consume as if we are free to consume as we wish. At the very same time we are told that we are living in a "consumer economy" and that the very health of the economy depends on individual consumers freely choosing to spend money. We've come to find out that we don't have as much choice as we suspected. If we *choose* to not spend, we're told we're a detriment to the economy and a bane to our neighbor's financial hopes.

I'm not sure if you caught it, but there was some significant debate in 2008 about savings. Some economists said things along the lines of, "Saving is good, but now is not the time to save. We're in a recession and we need people to spend." Businesses that rely on the routine of consumerism are all for this attitude. It was as if higher value was being placed on a dollar spent than a dollar saved. Unchecked spending had got us into this mess and the way out of it was . . . more spending.

A recent, clever-as-a-serpent development in spendthriftery is the mail-in rebate where the company whose product you are buying makes you spend your real money, then converts it into "money" you have to spend somewhere else, while saying you are getting your money back. We experienced this with AT&T in a different scenario. My wife had an accident at the beach during the summer. She was at Swami's (a famous local surf spot) checking out the tide pools with Phoebe when a rogue wave took them out. They went from hopping through puddles to swimming for their lives, and rescuing Leanne's purse. Needless to say, her cell phone got ruined. I went to plead my case to AT&T and it seemed like they were being kind by letting us renew Leanne's mobile plan early so that she would qualify for a basic free phone. It actually cost $40, but they promised to refund the money, which they did in the form of an AT&T Visa Gift Card. We had spent $40 but we'd received something that wasn't money in return. Perhaps there is a way to redeem the card for money but it's designed for you to go out and spend. That's the kind of money American-style consumerism likes. It's a new gold standard: money that people have to use to buy stuff.

Other economists during the recession have advocated thrift, acknowledging that never-ending spending had gotten the country into the recession mess in the first place. Economically speaking, the 100 Thing Challenge favors spending restraint. What kind of harm awaits the economy if lots of people limit their spending? Let me offer up my 100 Thing Challenge year as a case study.

So how damaging have I been to the economy since embarking on my 100 Thing Challenge? All of us have unique circumstances, and so everyone who did the 100 Thing Challenge would have a different effect on the economy. But let's see if I have done my little part to destroy the world.

It so happened that when I began my 100 Thing Challenge journey, I did it at the time I was selling my equity position in the company I started. ChristianAudio was run well by me and my business partners. After four years, I was able to sell my percentage of the company for three times my initial monetary investment. Likely I broke even if I took into consideration my sweat equity, but I also learned quite a bit over those four years and so became a more skilled worker and, I hope, a more thoughtful person.

In late 2008 when I sold my portion of ChristianAudio, it was obvious that the country was heading into a recession. At that same time I was gaining recognition for the 100 Thing Challenge and landed a book deal with what felt to me like a respectable advance. I could have used my capital gains from ChristianAudio and my book advance to avoid a day job for a while. Instead, I happily kept my position overseeing the Web site at Point Loma Nazarene University.

Thus, in the year of my 100 Thing Challenge, here are just some of the ways that our household economy contributed to the national economy. We paid off debt, saved, and invested, not loads of money, but a respectable amount. We gave charitably to our church, Plant with Purpose, and World Vision. We bought a few family items: a couple of chairs, lamps, and some curtains to spruce up our living room. We continued to drive our cars, paying for gas and getting the oil changed by the local mechanic. We continued to eat at In-N-Out Burger once, or maybe twice, a week. (If you are unlucky enough to live east of Las Vegas and don't know, In-N-Out is a remarkably fresh "fast food" joint. They use patties made from the meat of only one cow—I've heard that some fast-food hamburgers can be a combination of dozens of different cows, which makes me want to dry heave. In-N-Out cooks to order and cuts fries from real potatoes right in front of you. It's really good food.) We still occasionally hired people to clean our house and trim our yard. We, not often enough, paid a babysitter to watch the kids while Leanne and I went on dates, spending some money eating at local restaurants. Way more often than eating out, we went to Trader Joe's and bought groceries. We even got sick and went to the doctor, paying our copays. And those are just some of the ways in which we continued to contribute to the economy despite my 100 Thing Challenge simplicity.

But it could have been different. I could have taken the money from the sale of ChristianAudio, my book advance, and my humble salary at Point Loma Nazarene University and used it to lease a new Mercedes. I would have been acting economically irresponsibly, but I could have done it. I would have been risking the future of our household economy. I would have been driving around my daughters' college educations, their wedding funds, our grandchildren's inheritance, Leanne's and my retirement savings. But no one would have stopped me. (Except maybe Leanne.)

In fact, American-style consumerism encouraged me to make irresponsible economic decisions during my 100 Thing Challenge. I still received catalogs in the mail. I still saw advertisements online. I still saw commercials on TV, when we visited our parents' houses and watched television (we don't have one). And honestly, I was still tempted to buy stuff. Even luxury stuff.

But I made a commitment to resist. And that is the core economic point of the 100 Thing Challenge. I do not suggest that people stop participating in the economy. I am saying we should all resist taking part in American-style consumerism. What if everyone did?

What if everyone did the 100 Thing Challenge and used the

freedom from the incessant purchasing demanded by American-style consumerism for more profitable economic activity? What if we all stopped making foolish credit card purchases that functionally placed us in debtors' prison? What if, as a result of making do with fewer things, we prioritized buying better things that were a little more expensive and made by tradesmen instead of factory workers? What if we bought clothes from tailors instead of sweatshops? What if we stopped using our homes as storage facilities and decluttered the places in which we live so that they became sanctuaries from the daily grind instead of a never-ending hassle to clean?

To be honest, I don't know the empirical answer to those questions. If everyone did the 100 Thing Challenge and cut back their consumer spending by X percent, I do not know the Y percentage increase in savings or investment required to offset the decline in the sale of consumer goods. I just know what I believe is the intuitive and obvious answer: if everyone did the 100 Thing Challenge and as a result it helped them use their money and talents well, it would be good for the economy.

But let's turn the question around. What has happened when only one guy does the 100 Thing Challenge and tens of millions of other people spend like there's no tomorrow? What has been the result of mass participation in American-style consumerism? Well, in the relentless push to buy more stuff, we have pushed jobs out of the United States. Not just manufacturing jobs, either. Other kinds of skilled jobs from technologists to managers have been outsourced in order to create more efficiency so that prices can drop . . . wait for it . . . so that consumers can buy more stuff. We've traded jobs to China so that we can go to Walmart and buy a T-shirt made in China for $8.99, instead of paying $11.99 for that same T-shirt made in the United States. What a deal! We saved $3 and can now buy little Johnny that plastic race car (made in China) tantalizingly hanging on the shelf of the checkout aisle. Look, I've got nothing against China. I actually think they make some really good products. If they make things we call "cheap crap," it's only because there's a market for cheap crap. Let's be honest, that cheap crap market's name is "American-style consumerism."

We've built an economic system based on the endless acquisition of more and more. The *Oxford English Dictionary* defines "consumerism" as the "name given to a doctrine advocating a continual increase in the consumption of goods as a basis for a sound economy." How sound is our economy? There's been a housing meltdown. There's ten percent unemployment. (Actually, it would be considerably higher if the government counted the people who have given up looking for a job as unemployed instead of labeling them "discouraged workers.") Even with the recent uptick in personal savings rates, there's an enormous amount of personal debt. And public debt has ballooned to almost hopeless proportions.

Here's a thought experiment to finish up my rant. In your mind's eye, imagine the last time you drove by your neighbors' open garages. Were they empty? Now think about what you have in your garage. Is there stuff there? How much stuff is in the garages and closets and strewn across the front yards (he admits a little sheepishly) of your neighborhood? Do we all have enough stuff? Now think about it: Do we have a sound economy?

So to answer the question, if everyone took the 100 Thing Challenge and freed themselves from American-style consumerism, I firmly believe the result would be really positive. This is one case where I believe "more and more" is truly better.

THE 88 THING CHALLENGE

The first week in June, I did my inventory and found I had eighty-eight things. I had been somewhere in the nineties and had recently gotten rid of some clothes—a Gap sweater and an Old Navy button-down shirt—but I was planning to replace these items. Then a couple more clothing items were dropped off at Goodwill and, *bang*, I'm at eighty-eight things. Of course, there were occasionally some upward pressures too. I thought about buying a boogie board for Phoebe for her birthday and perhaps I'd also get myself a wetsuit. We live about ten miles from the ocean and we have fun messing around in it, so why not?

Our minds were definitely turned toward outdoor, or non-electronic, activities. I blogged about getting a boat. I grew a beard, a man's most passive activity. On June 15, Leanne and I decided that we'd turn off our computers Monday through Friday from 5 p.m. to 9 p.m. No Facebook, no e-mail, no Twitter. No chance of browsing a retail site because I wasn't going to be browsing anything. And I realized the kids didn't mind not having a computer as they busied themselves in other activities. (Eventually they tired of this rule and wanted to escape to the computer for some online games.) And I realized that the 100 Thing Challenge was putting me in the frame of mind where letting go of things, or habits, like mindlessly browsing the Internet, wasn't traumatic.

I took another thing off my list when Leanne and I gave up (for the moment at least) our proposed "Schooled in Marriage" podcast. She asked that I not get rid of the microphone in case we picked up the idea again later. But I didn't want to count something that I was perfectly content to return to the store. The 100

Thing Challenge lifestyle was getting comfortable. I was able to get something that I needed or get rid of something I didn't need without much worry one way or the other. I was able to adjust other aspects of life without fretting about it. Halfway through my challenge, I realized I had settled into it.

13. **My Almost Perfect Wednesday**

I had a ridiculously amazing day on Wednesday, August 5, 2009. I am using Southern California parlance. Around the Pacific Ocean here in San Diego the adverb "ridiculously" essentially means, in this context, "events came together so well that it was almost unbelievably great." It *was* a pretty unreal day.

The morning started with a surf. A couple months before my ridiculously amazing August 5, I had taken up surfing. As I mentioned earlier, despite being born and raised in San Diego, somehow I'd made it through thirty-seven years of life without ever attempting to learn. But now I was working at Point Loma Nazarene University, and my office was a forty-five-second car drive down a very steep three-hundred-foot hill to a dorm parking lot next to the water. Day after day I smelled the salty air and saw the beauty of the ocean. Day after day I watched the surfers paddling out to catch waves. Day after day my surfing coworker Marcus prodded me to give it a try. Eventually I gave in.

On June 24 in the year of my 100 Thing Challenge, Marcus let me borrow one of his boards and took me surfing. We went down to the water and stood on the beach looking west onto a break called the "In Betweens." He gave me a few tips and then we hit the waves. I laid myself down on the surfboard and stuck my arms in the water to move them, but it felt like I was paddling through Jell-O. It turns out that learning to stand up on a surfboard is the second of two very difficult skills I would have to learn. The first trial was figuring out how to propel myself through the water in order to get to the waves.

The allure of being in the ocean won out over the trauma of being shoulder sore and beaten down by waves. I persevered enough over the next month to learn to find my way around the ocean on a surfboard and to catch small waves and to stand up. In six weeks I was hardly a "surfer," though. Even so it was a delight to surf, despite the fact that I remained unsure of myself and unaware of all the dangers involved, such as cracking my head open on my surfboard. That's what I did one evening in late July as the sun was going down. It was hot and I hopped off my board to dunk my head under the water to cool off. Apparently, a swell pushed my board right back to where my head was coming out of the water. *Thump.* It didn't hurt. It didn't even seem like a hard hit. I didn't take notice for a few seconds, until I felt the warm blood gushing down the left side of my face. Five staples in my head later I had learned an important surfing lesson Marcus had forgotten to teach me: know where your surfboard is at all times and keep your head away from it.

The Monday before my almost perfect Wednesday, August 5, my doctor removed the staples and gave me her blessing to get back into the ocean. As you can imagine, I was a little tentative the first time paddling out again. But the point is that I started what was to become a ridiculously amazing day that Wednesday by surfing. After about an hour in the water, I turned around and headed back to shore. The sun had made its way up over the top of Sunset Cliffs and sparkled on the early morning breakers, kicking up a golden layer of steam that made the little cove where I got out of the water look ethereal. I felt like my day was starting in heaven on earth. The day started off well.

At work, all day long, things went great. No fires to put out. Pleasant and productive meetings. Some tasks accomplished. Cool ocean breeze blowing through my open office window. Friendly conversations around the water cooler. You know the kind of work day I am talking about: the kind when work isn't so bad.

And it kept getting better. Just after polishing off a delicious lunch of leftover teriyaki chicken, my wife called and let me know that she was *not* going to the circus with the kids that night. It turned out that my father-in-law, Billy, who relishes the circus, was going to take his wife, Cathy, instead of Leanne, to help with our kids. Out of nowhere came the makings of what tends to be all too elusive for couples with children: a date night.

I left for home a few minutes early, changed clothes, and we scurried off to Las Olas, a lovely Mexican restaurant that sits between San Elijo Lagoon and the Pacific Ocean in the laid-back beach town of Cardiff-by-the-Sea. The fish taco platter with rice and beans is, to say the least, delicious.

Now, I am writing toward a point about American-style consumerism. In a few paragraphs I will get there. But I need to be honest about my day or my words will not sound genuine. There was one primary hang-up on Wednesday the fifth, and it happened at Las Olas. We decided to splurge and get a side of guacamole with our chips and salsa. If you know anything at all about Mexican restaurants, then you know that they are notorious for skimping on their sides of guacamole. So when the waitress suggested we get the large, we figured it was a good recommendation—unfortunately it was not, unless there had been another Leanne and Dave. Wanting to get our eight dollars' worth, we ate about half the total guacamole serving—each of us likely ingesting two or three avocados. We definitely felt guacamole wobbly by the end of the meal. In fact, I am pretty sure that I pissed guacamole the next day. But overall, that was one minor irritation in the grand scheme of an otherwise excellent day.

Back to the positives. After our meal, we walked about thirty paces across the street to the warm sand of the beach and watched the sun drop past the horizon. It felt like we were falling in love all over again, except that we had been in love and happily married for thirteen years and so there wasn't any of the awkwardness of young love. It was a romantic and comfortable moment. We stood there chatting, bumping shoulders, and holding hands.

Then we drove back home, got cozy, and watched a movie on my laptop, Thomas Campell's surf film *The Present*. At that time it was the only surf movie I had seen besides the original, *The Endless Summer*, and it was pretty good. Leanne didn't even complain. We both agreed that Indonesia looked like an incredible place to visit. We laughed at the absurdity of the scene when Count Trimula rode a coffin rigged like a surfboard. And I marveled at the unbelievable African waves that broke perfectly for hundreds and hundreds of yards. But halfway through the flick my wife reminded me that we had not yet made love.

I turned off the computer.

About thirty minutes later the kids returned home from the circus thrilled beyond measure and tired as could be. We helped them into bed without much of a hitch. Then the whole family, dog, cat, and guinea pig included, fell asleep and rested soundly through the night. From 5:30 a.m. to 11:00 p.m., Wednesday the fifth was a ridiculously amazing day.

You might find satisfaction in different circumstances than I do. You just cannot deny, though, that a day like the one I have described, whatever the particulars, is a joy.

The pleasures of Wednesday the fifth required minimal consumer accessories. In fact, I feel comfortable asserting that if I had more—or more luxurious—consumer accessories, it would not have made the day any better. On Wednesday the fifth, I drove around in my sixteen-year-old Mazda 929 that had 122,000 miles on the engine. It worked just fine, except the radio turned off in the heat of the afternoon, like it does all afternoons. The radio usually stops working when the temperature hits around seventy-one degrees Fahrenheit. That only meant Leanne and I were not tempted to listen to music or NPR or the Padres lose while driving to Las Olas. Instead, we enjoyed a lively conversation with a healthy dose of well-meaning gossip about some friends.

Earlier in the day, my old Mazda got me to the ocean to surf pretty much as well as any car I could own. Sure, the back right tire had a nearly imperceptible slow leak, and every third time I filled the car up with gas I also added some air to the tire. But owning a car without this eccentric inconvenience would not impact the quality of the waves or make me a better surfer.

In the end, I used twenty personal things on Wednesday

the fifth. It took only *twenty* of my own things to have one of the
best days of my life:

1. old Mazda
2. surfboard
3. surf racks
4. wetsuit
5. plastic container to hold wet wetsuit in
   car trunk
6. water jug to wash off the ocean water
   after surf
7. laptop to watch surf movie (digital
   download)
8. mechanical pencil, which I used at my
   day job
9. cell phone
10. sunglasses
11. underwear
12. socks, until after work when I switched
    to sandals
13. shoes (see #12)
14. button-down shirt, until after work
    when I changed into a T-shirt
15. pants, until after work when I changed
    into shorts
16. sandals
17. T-shirt
18. shorts
19. wallet
20. wedding ring

What does it take to be happy? When Leanne and I were standing on the beach watching the sunset, a thought came to me: "We are living a nearly perfect day."

Sure, not everything went exactly right. The kids, no doubt, caused Leanne some stress at some point in the afternoon. I wished I could surf better. Something annoying must have happened at work that I have since forgotten about. We ate too much guacamole. Yet what more could a person on this earth want than a beautiful place to live, a connection with nature, a stable job, a healthy family, kind in-laws, a loving spouse, Mexican food, and sex? The prayer we said over our meal at Las Olas, thanking God for his provisions in our lives, was sane. It made sense to be thankful. We had been provided for.

∎ ∎ ∎

The crux of American-style consumerism is that our common lives lack provision. Somehow we have come to believe that there is always a purchase that will transform what is ridiculously amazing into what is perfect. I have lived too much of my life as if that were the case.

As if a sunset is more beautiful when I'm watching it while wearing the "right" brand of clothing. As if owning the right things would clarify my faith and make my hopes more real. As if possessions, instead of love, were the force that could knit my relationships together more tightly. As if the accomplishments of my life were largely about the stuff I use to get things done. I have lived too much of my life as if my experiences of the natural world, the realms of faith, the delights of love, and the satisfaction of work would all somehow be transformed from ridiculously amazing to perfect by something I pick out at a store.

That is the message of American-style consumerism. My human life is not enough. There are purchases upon purchases that will transform me into something more than what I am. We have too little tolerance for almost perfect Wednesdays.

Most of us have opportunities throughout our time on earth—right here and now—to soak up joy. Our lives are capable of accommodating pleasures beyond our wildest imaginations. Our minds can process and our souls can nurture abundant joy. But I have deceived myself and drained my hopes and frustrated my relationships and busted my ass striving for perfect days. Days not meant for any creature, not even a human like me, who can shop.

MY 10 THING HOBBY

Perhaps the most significant thing I added to the list in the later months of the challenge was my lightly used 7′ 3″ TDK surfboard. When I bought it I couldn't surf at all but I persevered. Cracking my head open on the board and having the laceration in my scalp stapled shut didn't help me with a general bout of summer malaise that hit at the end of July. And I broke my trusty altimeter watch by shutting it in the trunk of my car not once but twice. I wanted to replace it but took an age to do so, fretting about spending the money. I eventually bought a replacement, an inferior watch without the altimeter, on sale.

My head injury kept me out of the water for a couple weeks. What surprised me most was my eagerness to get back in and have another go at it. A couple times I seriously thought about ditching my doctor's advice and paddling out with the staples still lodged in my head. I decided this was positive, rather than foolish, motivation. Surfing was hard and it seemed like it would take me months to get the hang of it, but I never contemplated not giving it a thorough try.

At first I had just the two things: a wetsuit and a surfboard. Surfing seemed to fit the 100 Thing Challenge perfectly but I quickly realized I'd need some more stuff. How much of a slippery slope was this? Because my full-body wetsuit felt like an electric blanket turned to high in the warmer summer waters, I bought a wetsuit jacket to wear with board shorts. Then I added a second pair of board shorts. I also commandeered a storage bin and a water jug, to keep my car trunk from getting wet and to wash the ocean water out of my hair, respectively. And I installed soft racks for carrying my board on top of my car, though I learned that if I open a couple of the doors just right and turn the board on its side and push really hard, I can cram it into my car. I probably don't technically need the racks.

So eventually, eight personal possessions were devoted to surfing and it seemed like a lot to me. I got the sense that it wouldn't be hard to double that in one weekend surf shop outing. For some reason, ten things seems like a good number for a hobby, even though I don't really practice what I preach here. I have more than ten camping items. How many items does it take you to enjoy your favorite hobby? I had more thoughts I posted on my blog:

A final thought about surfing and stuff. I am desiring a new surfboard already. Well, sort of. I desire to work hard at getting better so that I can ride a smaller, more fun board. The idea of riding something more capable than my current board is one motivation. It's not the only or the main thought that gets me back in the water each time.

But it crosses my mind. And I have
to admit that striving for a goal that
includes a new personal possession
has some appeal. It feels dangerous to
me, though. Like it would be possible to
start wanting the thing more than what
the thing is for.

I stuck with the surfing and at the end of September had
a breakthrough. I paddled out and caught the first wave that I
can actually say I surfed. No falling over after a few seconds. No
riding mush straight to the beach. Nothing fancy. It was a right
(meaning the wave broke to the right) that was a bit more than
waist high. Even so, I caught it, turned down the line, and rode
the thing. I even managed a slow-motion cutback that would have
impressed a sea slug. True to form, I didn't leave the water unin-
jured. I was surfing a little south of my normal spot and didn't
know the reef there and I managed to cut my foot a little bit,
though it was nothing too bad.

14. A Modest Proposal for the One Thing We Should All Keep

I kept one pen throughout the year of my 100 Thing Challenge. It wasn't a twenty-five-cent Bic ballpoint pen, but it wasn't anything special, either. Over the year, maybe a few dozen times total, when I was away from my home or some family member misplaced my pen for a time, I used a different pen. It is remarkable how few pens a person needs. But I used to believe that I required lots of pens. Fancy pens.

For a time in my life I actually collected fancy pens. One pen I owned was a sterling silver pen from Tiffany & Co. My parents gave it to me (either for Christmas or my birthday, I forget), knowing that I was going through a time in my life when I appreciated elegant writing instruments. If I recall right, my dad picked it out. The pen was heavy, well balanced, and I liked it.

My desire to possess an heirloom-quality pen accompanied a fantasy I regularly had at the time. As a young businessman almost thirty years old, I would imagine myself many years later sitting behind a large desk, completing a particularly difficult negotiation. Between the other person and me, on the surface of the desk, rested the final contract. We sat uncomfortably quiet for several minutes.

Finally, I stirred in my chair. Reaching out my arm, I opened a drawer and withdrew a pen—a fancy pen. After I received it, sometimes I imagined it was that shiny Tiffany & Co. sterling silver pen. I looked at it. I looked at the person across from me.

"This pen is special," I enunciated softly.

Then I looked again at the pen, this time historically. As if the silver of the pen were a charmed mirror that reflected every business moment from my past, I sat there witnessing again all the agreements that pen had signed. Where it had taken me and my business. The bonds it had created or scribbled away.

"The drawer is empty except for the pen," I said, returning to the moment. There was a subtle, though not to be reckoned with, rumble in my voice. "You need to understand that I do not open this drawer and remove this pen until I am ready."

Now, looking into the person's eyes and speaking like granite, "When I use this pen to sign my name, *I* am ready. Take a moment, please." I pause like I am smoking a cigar. "Are you prepared to enter into this agreement?"

Sometimes in my fantasy the person just breaks down. I have pity, like feeling sorry for a runt dog.

Braver negotiators choke out, "Yes." They cannot hold my stare, though. And they sign the contract with a trembling hand.

Then every so often, a courageous business partner with fortitude to match mine nods his head, leans forward, and signs his name. His face is stoic, but his soul has broken out into a smile, sitting across from his newly discovered kindred spirit. We are both thinking, "There are so few of us."

Embarrassing but true.

I have no recollection if, in real life, that sterling silver pen from Tiffany & Co. ever signed an agreement of any magnitude. I am pretty sure that I used it to sign several of the contracts for ChristianAudio. Perhaps it also signed the corporate minutes that bound us business partners together, sometimes ruefully. If it did, its stroke was temporary. I've already shared how I moved on from ChristianAudio, selling my position in the company for less than it was probably worth, unable to navigate the financial burdens, vocational complexities, and relational strains of entrepreneurialism. You have to wonder about the efficacy of elegant writing instruments with nonpermanent ink.

It doesn't matter anyway. By the time I was using it for ChristianAudio work, the silver on that Tiffany & Co. pen had grown blemished and had begun to chip. For years it looked like a hand-me-down, not an heirloom. Clearly, it was the wrong pen.

So I collected different pens. A hand-turned exotic wood pen. A skinny French pen. A blue Italian pen. A retractable fountain pen. The ubiquitous Montblanc pen. And I looked admiringly at other fancy pens—hundreds of them, at stores and online. Every time I wondered what a new pen might accomplish. What deal it might sign. What life twist might spill from its nib.

Throughout my time on earth, with remarkable consistency, my dreams and aspirations have been lamely juxtaposed with my personal possessions. When I have been bold enough to reach beyond myself—to "reach for the stars"—invariably I have managed to stay on terra firma. Then I go to the store and buy things in a puny mortal effort to grab at more than I can

get on my own. Really, what is a sparkly sterling silver pen compared to intimidation?

Well, that is not really what I am after in my life anyway,
being feared by others, even on account of my upscale accessories. I confirmed that during my 100 Thing Challenge. The
fancy-pen phase of my life was relatively brief and uncomfortable, never quite the right fit for who I am or, at least, who I wish
to be. It was pretty easy to get rid of the pens.

I have found that I sometimes used stuff this way. I have
held a fancy pen in my hand as if it were a chisel and I was both
the rock and the sculptor.

Often I have grabbed hold of my possessions and started
hammering. Somehow I have thought that fancy pens could
knock away at my circumstances and shape me into a rough-
and-tumble businessman. Or toy trains could refashion my
youth. Or gear and adventuring could chip away until a perfectly content and secure soul took form. Or woodworking tools
could manufacture a life of confidence. Maybe my sculpting
handiwork could turn me into someone bigger and more com-
petent than I am. Someone who could grasp at things beyond
my reach.

Even though I am relatively handy with woodworking tools,
it's like I have two left thumbs when I use my possessions for
life work, when I use my stuff to make me better. I am so weak
and incapable. I'm like poor old Job, who after all his misery was
questioned by God: "Can you bind the chains of the Pleiades or
loose the cords of Orion?" Righteous though he was, Job could
not meddle with the stars. Neither can I.

But there is more to weakness than the actual limitations of
our humanity. If I am powerless to reach beyond myself, I nevertheless am fanciful and all too often give it a shot. Of course

I have failed. It is just that unlike Job, who fell silent before his distance from the heavens, I have attempted to extend my reach across impossible realms. I have looked through stores for accessories I can buy to get me up there.

I think there is a reason I have regularly used stuff to bridge the space between who I am and who I think I would like to be. It is not just that I am personally not cut out to be a threatening businessman who amasses fortunes. Whether that is a noble goal for anyone, the fact is that some people are capable of it. People are able to reach different levels of what we call "accomplishment." Yet there are limits, for me and for each of us. We cannot bind the chains of the Pleiades. The stars are out of our *human* reach. I have not always wanted to admit that. So too the dream life, branded and sold by American-style consumerism, is beyond the stretch of our human hands. I have not always been willing to submit to that truth, either. The dream life we find at malls is not a dream, as in a realistic hope, which we could put our faith in. The dream life accessorized by American-style consumerism is a fancy, an immature urge outside the purview of truth. It is the dream to go after what is not ours to have and what we could not get anyway.

We can pursue the dream life of American-style consumerism, but only by relentlessly getting more possessions and using them to try to be more than we actually are. We must keep it up, because they will always fail to make us completely satisfied. We must continually ask our things to make us happy. And we unavoidably place heavy demands on people and the world when we live like that.

"We have, in fact, no right to ask the world to conform to our desires," writes Wendell Berry. "Sooner or later, if we hope to grow up, we have to confront the opposite imperative: that our rights and the realization of our desires are limited by human nature, by human community, and by the nature of the places in which we live."*

Who is going to do that? Are we going to choose to limit our rights? Is American-style consumerism going to encourage that? What catalog sells the humility we'd need in order to acknowledge our personal limits, acquiesce to neighborliness, and nurture the environment instead of try to dominate it?

The truth is that our material possessions, rather than helping us understand our limits and our place in the world, regularly distort our perspective. Put a Coach purse or the key to a BMW M series or the latest Nokia gadget in our hands and it's not uncommon for humility, respect for other people, and appreciation of our environment to drain from our brains.

◾ ◾ ◾

The noisiest and least dignified I've ever been in a public restroom was in Seattle's Sea-Tac Airport. It happened early in my 100 Thing Challenge year, when I was traveling through Seattle from Helena, Montana, after the speaking engagement I've already told you about. The layover on the flight back was long, and I had plenty of time for a hearty meal. As I mentioned, I had been sick in Montana and was now suffering from horrible postnasal drip. At least for me, a bellyful of coffee, French toast, scrambled eggs, maple bacon, and hot snot makes for an uncomfortable and loud visit to the bathroom. I should have known better when I was ordering breakfast. But once I'd made the mistake there was nothing to be done about it.

Leaving my pride in the airport terminal, I sat in a stall and

---

* Wendell Berry, *Another Turn of the Crank* (Washington, D.C.: Counterpoint, 1995), 83–84.

got down to business. Next to me was a man doing his extremely noisy deed. And on the other side of him was yet another person refusing to be upstaged by the two of us. Tchaikovsky would have been impressed. It sounded like a redneck version of the 1812 Overture, with twelve-gauge shotguns replacing the cannons. All the while, the guy in the stall nearest to me was on his cell phone shouting out strategies for a business meeting he was planning with a *female* coworker!

"For the love of all that is industrious," I thought, "could this possibly be what Adam Smith had in mind?"

It's hard to imagine such absurd behavior without access to a mobile device that is so packed full of features that we are conditioned to take it everywhere. Surely this man, in a precellular era, wouldn't have invited his colleague into the bathroom with him for this planning session. (Even the thought of that gives me the willies.) It only makes sense that a businessman cannot wait five minutes to make a call when he's operating under the assumption that the thing he is holding allows him to transcend normalcy. He can be more than a human being who has to pause from time to time to defecate. He can be a man who can poop and conduct business at the same time. American-style consumerism, the things it produces and the frenetic lifestyle it requires of us, has not bridged the gap from earth to our heavenly dreams, it has destroyed the natural barriers safeguarding us from our proclivity to embarrass ourselves.

The irony of it all is that as we embrace American-style consumerism we become fools, thus humiliating ourselves. Wouldn't it be better to just be humble in the first place? I have just the answer: the 100 Thing Challenge. I had abundant opportunities to practice humility during the year of my 100 Thing Challenge.

Like in September 2009, just before the 100 Thing Challenge ended, when I was invited to speak at Pathways Community Church in San Diego. It was a casual church, so I wore jeans and sandals. As Pastor Phil called me to the stage, I climbed up the steps and looked down, only to realize too late that I was wearing capris! The jeans had been washed so many times over the year that they had shrunk a couple inches. Why had I not seen it before? There I was, standing in front of two hundred smiling faces, all looking at my hairy ankles. You know what? I was a little self-conscious up there but no one really cared. There are more important things than the way we look on the outside. It was a great night. Pastor Phil and his congregation were warm and welcoming. The conversations afterward, inspiring. I even ran into an old friend, Larry, whom I'd not seen in over a decade. The night was proof positive that, contrary to popular opinion, one doesn't always have to dress for success.

I learned humility in other ways too. Without woodworking tools, I needed something to do with my hands on the weekends. I decided to sledgehammer our tiny backyard patio and make a vegetable garden, which Leanne and the girls had wanted for some time. Even though my father is a master gardener and I grew up around a beautiful suburban vegetable patch in the backyard, I never acquired a green thumb. Our garden was a sweaty chore to put in. It wasn't perfect. The tomatoes took off like Jack's beanstalk but the beans themselves withered and died no matter what I did. And then there was the rat. It crept out of its hole at night and chewed up the tomatoes. Its little rat teeth made quiet nibbling noises that we could hear through our open bedroom window on hot summer evenings. He made me want to become a consumer again, so I could buy a pellet gun. We never caught that darn pest—one time our cat Beatrice cornered it but it managed to escape. Piper still sniffs the area of the garden where the tomatoes were planted.

The whole experience was quite humbling. But the garden and the rat were also exciting and provided endless laughter and storytelling among friends. I really doubt I'd have planted that garden if I'd still been piddling away in the garage not doing much real woodworking on the weekends.

Then there were the more subtle moments of humility. The times when I wasn't embarrassed by my clothing frugality or exasperated by my simple-life hobbies like gardening, but when I looked on my ordinary human life with a fresh 100 Thing Challenge perspective. One summer night Leanne and I went to dinner at a little Italian restaurant near our home. The food was great and we scarfed it down, then sat impatiently waiting for the bill. The waitress was taking her time, slowly moving from one table to the next, chatting, filling up water glasses, suggesting desserts. It dawned on us. We weren't in a rush. We had no plans to eat and run off to Target or Home Depot or browse a mall, like we had done so many other times in our dating life. The feeling of taking our time, relishing our meal without the need to be aware of the hour so that we didn't finish after the stores closed, felt unusual to us. It was an uneasy realization, if not an exactly humiliating one.

Learning humility doesn't have to be humiliating. I like what Dallas Willard, a philosopher at the University of Southern California, says about the humble life: "To be humble simply means to be realistic about yourself."*

Wow! I was actually able to do that.

Well, I mean, not entirely. Yet after this preposterous simple

* Dallas Willard, Wheaton College, chapel address, April 17, 2009.

living project I named the 100 Thing Challenge, I was able to get a better grip on what's possible. After all the fancy pens, the trains, and the woodworking tools were gone. After all the phantasmal things were purged from my life. After I got used to living without much stuff and was able to rest without buying new things. After all that, I got a better view of a more realistic life than the dream life of American-style consumerism.

I ended the year no longer a slave to my stuff. Abundance didn't clutter my perception of myself. And we could finally park Leanne's minivan in the garage to boot! The 100 Thing Challenge was subversive and empowering. It defied the logic of American-style consumerism, which insists that we need more and more things to be content. Unshackled from my stuff, the 100 Thing Challenge gave me the required physical and emotional space to get what I—what we all—really need, more of this marvelous never-quite-entirely-but-almost-perfect life.

Epilogue

Keep Going

My 100 Thing Challenge is over and I am not going to continue following its rules. Yet I intend to thoughtfully and joyfully press on.

The truth is that I have been tempted to keep going with the 100 Thing Challenge. The process of freeing myself from the restraints of American-style consumerism has been so fantastically energizing, I just do not want to stop living it. But maturity involves growing from one stage in life to another. The 100 Thing Challenge was never meant to be a lifelong project. It served a purpose. The purpose of the 100 Thing Challenge was to help me break free from the confining nature of American-style consumerism. It was meant to be a way for me, a person who felt stuck in stuff, to get out. It was a jailbreak. The plan has always been that, so long as all went well with the 100 Thing Challenge, I would not need to keep breaking free. And it has gone well. So what's next?

Some months have passed between the official end to my 100 Thing Challenge on November 12, 2009, and now, when I am sitting down to finish my book by writing this epilogue. In that time, my 100 Thing Challenge has remained popular and continued to gain participants. A lot of regular people from around the world have become fans of the 100 Thing Challenge page on Facebook. Hundreds follow it on Twitter. Dozens have been bold enough to contact me directly. And some recognizable names preaching simple living have embarked on it, such as Leo of zenhabits.net—though he is twice as impressive a minimalist as me, having reduced his 100 Thing Challenge to a 50 Things (plural) Challenge.

(This is as good a place as any for me to point out that officially it is the "100 Thing (singular) Challenge" not the "100 Things (plural) Challenge." I chose to use the singular for a couple reasons. The singular is grammatically incorrect, which makes it more memorable. It just sounds better in the singular. Also, as I'm sure you know by now, the 100 Thing Challenge isn't really about "things." It is not about changing what we own so much as changing the way in which we acquire what we own. The 100 Thing Challenge is more about resisting American-style consumerism than it is about resisting things in general. The "thing" I'm trying to get rid of is stupid consumption. The way I personally did that was to live with a minimal amount of things long enough for me to break my dumb consumer habits.)

Whether I use the singular or others, like Leo, use the plural, it has become apparent to me that despite my doubts and my friend Andy's prophecy, the 100 Thing Challenge will last for some time to come. Throughout the year of my 100 Thing Challenge and now, after it is officially over for me, one of the greatest pleasures I've received from the experience is watching as other people co-opt it and modify it in personal ways, making it their own challenge. A grassroots movement needs some diversity to spread and thrive. I'm delighted that the 100 Thing Challenge has been sustained by others and will exist after me. Keep going!

. . .

On a personal note, the 100 Thing Challenge has brought me to a better place. The 100 Thing Challenge itself is not a better place. It is a narrow doorway, which I discovered isn't easy to find or get through. What I have learned, though, is that the tight squeeze of the 100 Thing Challenge opens up to far greater possibilities than the unmistakable double-wide doors that comfortably lead into stores. It is a cinch to enter through those big doors, but there's only so far you can go once inside. I prefer the harder challenge of the smaller door that opens to expansive opportunities.

Of course, I have to be honest and tell you that I don't know all that is on the other side of the 100 Thing Challenge. But what kind of person would want to know everything that is to come? Not a very adventurous person, I should think.

I do know that I am no longer a slave to stuff. I know that although I continue to buy things and do my part in the economy, I am no longer a participant in the reckless and hopeless cycle of American-style consumerism. And I know that the 100 Thing Challenge has afforded me the great privilege of connecting with many people the world over who want their lives to be more valuable than the sum of their material possessions. I'm inspired by them!

I have come to call my post–100 Thing Challenge future my

Little Goods Life. It's a pun. Even though I will not follow the exact rules of the 100 Thing Challenge anymore, I am continuing to live a life of "little consumer goods." I am not, and have no intention of, rushing out and buying loads of new things. I'm not replacing the pens. I'm not starting up a toy train collection again. I didn't add to my adventure gear—with the exception of one more pocket knife—until I decided to add a handful of things for a climb of Mount Whitney. But since the temperature was in the thirties, I figured it was better to get a few items than die. I'm not getting more things for surfing. In fact, the wildest result of the 100 Thing Challenge to date is that several months after finishing it, I still have fewer than one hundred things.

I am no longer living the official 100 Thing Challenge, but I am living with the ongoing influence of it. I continue to do this because resisting American-style consumerism is a necessary discipline for me to live a life of simplicity. The physical and spiritual space of this simple life gives me the room I need to pursue "little meaningful goods" in all the things I do. I am not trying to hit a charitable home run that fixes all the world's ills. I want to do my little part to move runners around the bases. I want people to look at me and be grateful that there's another human being who cares about them and the world.

The 100 Thing Challenge ended my efforts to strive for perfection and satisfaction at the mall. And I'm not much interested in being completely content in my pursuit of a meaningful life. I want to be really good at being a thoughtful and joyful person. We are not totally perfect and we're not always satisfied. Little by little, prioritizing everyday deeds and conventional relationships, I plan to keep going in what I am grateful to say is a ridiculously amazing life. Isn't that all anyone really needs?

Yes, that is enough.

Appendix 1

How to Do a 100 Thing Challenge

O n the face of it, doing a 100 Thing Challenge would seem pretty straightforward. Get rid of all but one hundred of your personal possessions and then live that way for a year. In reality, however, there's a bit more preparation required. In this appendix, I'd like to walk you through some recommendations for doing a 100 Thing Challenge of your own. And I'd like to share with you some of the practical lessons learned, hopefully to help you avoid some of the pitfalls that befell me.

Remind Me, Why Do a 100 Thing Challenge?
I have this fear. It's a Facebook fear. Someday after this book has been published, a person finds me on Facebook and friends me. He doesn't seem weird, so I accept. And by accepting, my new friend has access to my e-mail address. And he e-mails me about my book and the 100 Thing Challenge. And I reply

saying, "Thanks," forgetting to remove my e-mail signature, which includes my mobile number. And then I get a call.

It's him and he's mad as hell. He tells me how his wife read about the 100 Thing Challenge and decided to do it. And she forced him to do it. And the kids to do it. And the dog and cat to do it. And now he's blaming me!

So let me just reiterate, doing a 100 Thing Challenge is not for everyone. Not every person should combat American-style consumerism by living with only one hundred personal possessions for an extended period of time. If it's not a fit for you or your family, please don't do it.

But a 100 Thing Challenge is just the ticket some people need. Some people feel "stuck in stuff" and need to get away from consumerism. For some of these people, doing a 100 Thing Challenge can be a catalyst to get them moving again, on the way to a better life. If you are one of those people who thinks that a 100 Thing Challenge might do the trick, how can you confirm your hunch? That's the first thing to do when considering a move like this. Make sure you know that the 100 Thing Challenge is for you.

I've developed a two-question quiz that is a surefire way to evaluate if a 100 Thing Challenge is a good fit for you.

Question 1: Are you bothered on a daily basis by the fact that you have too much stuff?

Question 2: Really?

If your answer to those two questions is yes, then you should consider doing a 100 Thing Challenge. If you said no then it might be best for you to hold off.

But let's say you said, "Yes, I want to do a 100 Thing Challenge of my own." You'll need to determine why you're going to put yourself through the stress and social awkwardness, but also the joys, of resisting American-style consumerism. You'll need to keep the "Why?" in front of you throughout your journey. It's going to get tough. And you'll need to remind yourself of what you're trying to accomplish. There can be many valid reasons to do a 100 Thing Challenge: to help manage finances better, to declutter, to break a bad shopping habit. All of those played a part in my decision to do the 100 Thing Challenge. Mostly, though, I wanted to be freed from the pressures of always feeling like I needed to get stuff to become content.

Once you have decided to go for it, always remember it's your challenge. I came up with my own list of rules (and exceptions) that made it challenging but doable for me. My rules aren't a blueprint; they might not feel right for you. So come up with your own rules. Perhaps one hundred things are too few, but that's not a deal breaker. If you live in a house twice the size of mine and have twice as much stuff as I used to have, then a 200 Thing Challenge is proportionately just as difficult but will also push back against American-style consumerism. Other people may feel that I am a hopeless lotus eater luxuriating in my hundred things and will want to live for a year with fifty or twenty-five or ten things. As far as challenges go, one size does not fit all.

In an effort to make my critique of American-style consumerism pithy, I came up with a three word tagline for the 100 Thing Challenge: *Reduce. Refuse. Rejigger.* This provides a nice structure for outlining my recommendations for doing your own 100 Thing Challenge.

How to Reduce

Here is what I recommend you do to start preparing for your 100 Thing Challenge. Go into your closet and get one week's worth of clothing. Make sure you have a different, complete outfit for each day of the week: seven full outfits. Do something to your closet to section off these clothes. For the next couple of weeks, they are going to be all you wear. (Yes, you are going to wear the same clothes for two weeks in a row. Maybe more. Trust me, you're going to be wearing the same clothes a lot.)

I think it's best to start with clothes for two reasons. First, most people I've met believe that their wardrobe is what would hold them back from doing the 100 Thing Challenge. They tell me, "I could get down to two purses, but I could never get below one hundred clothing items." So my recommendation is to prove yourself wrong from day one. Start by showing yourself that for two weeks you really can dress comfortably and look dignified with thirty-five to forty clothing items. Second, everyone who thinks about doing the 100 Thing Challenge has too many clothes. And I mean *everyone*. All those clothes are a distraction. You cannot think about getting rid of the two walking sticks you craved when you were in Girl Scouts twenty years ago when you're standing numbly in your closet trying to figure out what to wear to work. You'll need space in your brain when the purging starts in earnest. You can free up a lot of emotional volume by getting rid of the burden of your closet-loads of stuff. Besides, you'll come back to your wardrobe later and make final adjustments to what you keep.

Once you know what you'll be wearing, it's time to identify what you'll be throwing out. (I recommend selling, donating, or giving away your stuff. In fact, I think one of the best things you can do is give your stuff to people you know. I'll come back to that point in a moment.) Some declutter experts have a very different opinion about this than me: they say you should just start chucking stuff. Get rid of it. All of it. Do a huge purge all at once. I'm not a declutter professional, so I'm not sure if that's sound advice, but it doesn't sound good to me.

I recommend identifying zones. You've already been in one zone, your closet, which you're going to return to. Cordon off other zones in your house or apartment: bedroom, bathroom, living room, office, garage. Then tackle them one at a time. There's an enormous feeling of accomplishment when something is all done. It's not likely that you are going to finish purging for your 100 Thing Challenge in one weekend. But you can purge your bathroom in one weekend. Task complete. Goal accomplished. See, you're on a roll!

At some point you'll need to start making a list of what you think you'll want to keep. My feeling is that you shouldn't do this until you're a few weeks into your purge. This will allow you to get rid of things you would have otherwise put on your "keep" list. By the time you get around to making the list and the thing has already been gone for a week or two, you'll have proven to yourself that you can live comfortably without it. Sure, you might have mild regret, but you'll be teaching yourself that you can live through disappointment. You will need to learn that lesson.

It took me a solid year to reduce my things to fewer than one hundred. I don't think it has to take that long. Hopefully you aren't as busy as I was back then, juggling a business and a day job and a family of three young daughters—and, of course, the unanticipated worldwide interest in the 100 Thing Challenge. But busy or not, this is serious stuff. If you think you can take care of any life change in a weekend, you're setting yourself up for failure. You're talking about changing your consumer behavior for a lifetime. That might take more than a few days.

So what do you keep?

You're not defined by your stuff. I felt liberated and freed when I unburdened myself. I felt more alive and happier, not diminished and lonely. So don't agonize over it. Only a few things are truly irreplaceable, and even those are not always something you want to keep, like an overbearing piece of ugly Victorian furniture. If something is irreplaceable and you'd be sad if you never saw it again, that's a good argument for keeping hold of it.

Where should you unload all these things you're purging? I had garage sales, used eBay and Craigslist, and donated items to Goodwill. But I think the best thing I did with my stuff was to give it to friends. It's enjoyable to give things away, and the pleasure of giving is magnified when you know the person who's receiving the gift. It will also force you to remain committed. The more things you give to people you know, the more often you will have to explain why you are giving your stuff away, and the more people in your life will be able to help you stay accountable. Who knows? Maybe one of them will decide to join you in the 100 Thing Challenge.

How to Refuse

Are you a praying person? If not, you might want to start once you begin your 100 Thing Challenge. It isn't easy to resist the temptations of American-style consumerism. Barring divine help, I've identified two sources of stuff acquisition you'll need to be sensitive to during your 100 Thing Challenge: other people and all stores. Not much to avoid there, eh?

You know how we preach tolerance in our culture? Well,

what I have found is that tolerance doesn't count when it comes to material possessions. If you have a relative who likes to give you gifts, that person isn't going to tolerate your decision to avoid stuff. If you have a boss at work who thinks the latest fashions are a sign of professional competence, that boss isn't going to tolerate your decision to wear the same clothes month after month. (Fortunately, I had neither in my life, though there were other challenging people.) You need to mentally steel yourself to stand firm in your conviction to take the 100 Thing Challenge. You're going to make other people uncomfortable. In an effort to combat their feelings of awkwardness, they are going to try to change your mind. Be ready for it.

Some people who don't interpret your 100 Thing Challenge as a personal attack are nevertheless going to think you're ignorant. They are going to feel no hint of restraint when the urge comes over them to make fun of you and tell you what a stupid waste of time your 100 Thing Challenge is. You could, of course, point out what ill-mannered dumbasses they are. But you're more dignified than that. My recommendation is to just grin and bear it. If someone persists in being a jerk, then purge him or her, too.

You will also need to avoid malls. There are two reasons to avoid malls and strip malls (remember that Target is always in a strip mall). That's where all the stores are. But there's another more amazing reason. It's the sense you will get when you inevitably have to go into a mall again. I spent six months without walking into a mall. When I returned to one with Leanne it was like going to Jupiter. Seriously, even if you don't do the 100 Thing Challenge, I challenge you to stay out of all malls for a year and then go back. You'll walk around with your jaw dropped, marveling at the absurdity of American-style consumerism.

Just like friends and family are not going to leave you alone when they learn you're doing the 100 Thing Challenge, marketers and advertisers are not going to leave you alone either. My feeling is that the very best way to refuse stuff is to avoid getting the stuff pitched to you in the first place. You know what this means, right?

Get rid of your television!

We've gone almost fourteen years without a television. We watch movies on our computer. We even watch TV shows, like *Wipeout*, from time to time on the computer. But there's no need to have a television, unless you have a need for hundreds of millionaires to spend billions of dollars to try to get you to buy thousands of things. You've got better things to do with your time and your money!

How to Rejigger

When I was thinking up my philosophy of simplicity, I tried to find three alliterative words. Obviously anyone doing the 100 Thing Challenge needs to reduce. And once down to one hundred or fewer things, a person doing the challenge needs to refuse to get more stuff. But what was the third "R"? After a thesaurus search, I discovered the perfect triplet completer, "rejigger." It means to reorganize or rearrange something. And that's just what you're doing when you take on the 100 Thing Challenge. You are organizing your material possessions differently and rearranging your lifestyle. Beating back American-style consumerism with the three "Rs" is hard work, but it can be done.

What is your rejiggered life going to look like when you're done with your 100 Thing Challenge? It will look different from almost anyone else's, at least in the particulars. Yet it might appear remarkably similar to the lives of those who prioritize a meaningful life over buying stuff. Your house will not be so cluttered. You will not feel pressured to keep up with the Joneses. You will have more time to enjoy the people you care about, since you will not be wasting time managing all your possessions, which, by the way, don't give a rip about you.

Of course, I thought a lot about how I wanted my life to benefit from the 100 Thing Challenge. In the epilogue, I shared my idea of the Little Goods Life, a lifestyle characterized by owning few consumer "goods" and also by doing many meaningful "goods." Figure out something like that for your newfound freedom from American-style consumerism. Don't take the extra time and energy you've established for yourself and use it to conquer the universe in some massive multiplayer online game. I mean, if you want to play the odd video game or two, go ahead. Games are fun. Just make sure your rejiggered priorities are focused on making the real world a better place and the real people around you feel cared for.

And keep going!

Appendix 2

Post-Challenge Things

In February 2010, after my 100 Thing Challenge had been over for a few months, a thought came to me: I wonder what I want now? I had been living for over a year with fewer than one hundred personal possessions and, now that I could, I wondered if I wanted more. So I sat down to create an "ideal" hundred things list. Here are some takeaways from that exercise.

Even though I am an advocate for simple living, I understand that I am still human and like to own things. Like most men, I like electronic gadgets. Like all people, I prefer to dress in nice clothes. Just because I'm the 100 Thing Challenge guy doesn't mean that I'm completely uninterested in stuff. Yet when I went to create my post–100 Thing Challenge list, I was shocked that it came in at a scant ninety-eight things. I thought hard about the list, asking myself to not worry about having too many things on it. "Just put down what you feel like you'd want," I told myself. Apparently the lessons of the 100 Thing Challenge stuck with me.

On this new list I did not include some items that were on my original list. For example, I did not include the desk, desk chair, side table, and iMac computer. I didn't include those items because I don't really use them, and when I do, it is definitely for shared purposes. These days, my wife gets far more use out of the desk and iMac than I do. I use the desk and desktop computer occasionally when I'm doing the bills and too lazy to open my laptop to check our bank statements.

But the new list included many new things. For example, I added a second pocket knife. A larger one, also by Benchmade, which makes delightfully well-crafted knives. In fact, I got that new knife in March 2010. So the new list included two knives. It also included a new camera, lens, and tripod to replace my point-and-shoot camera that I kept for the original 100 Thing Challenge. But I have not bought the new camera yet, and perhaps never will. I'd also like to someday replace my altimeter watch, which I miss. But I've already replaced my cell phone with an iPhone and bought the MotionX-GPS app, which has an excellent altimeter, along with many other great outdoor adventure features. I put a replacement acoustic guitar on my ideal list and got one, another Breedlove. I'd like to get some new hiking boots and a replacement pair of trail running shoes. My rain jacket needs replacing since it's a little worn out and leaky. I sure wish I had my old J.Crew jacket (the one made by elves) back, too. And I'd like quite a few new clothing items, maybe a dozen in all, for work. All told, I owned only eighty things as of March 2010. And there were eighteen things on my ideal list that I had not bought yet.

Perhaps this ideal list experiment should not have surprised me. But somehow it did. I figured I'd loosen up a little bit post–100 Thing Challenge and comfortably work my way up to 150 things. But as I thought about getting new stuff, I just couldn't put even hypothetical things on my list. For example, I added and then removed a bike. I love bikes. I like riding bikes. And objectively speaking, I should probably own a bike and helmet and biking shoes and accessories. It's just that I couldn't imagine using it much. It would likely sit in our garage week after week. I'd take it on camping trips and use it maybe one or two times then. I'd pull it out every couple weeks to tool around the street with my kids. Maybe I'll get a bike. Probably not.

There are probably some things that I'll get someday that didn't make it on my ideal list. I went fly-fishing in April 2010. Fly-fishing is a marvelous use of time and stuff. Fishing, even though I don't do it often enough, might be the best activity that a person can do with stuff. I could see buying fly-fishing gear, if I stumbled into a lifestyle that had time for fly-fishing. My oldest daughter wants to take up archery. I'll probably have to get her a bow and arrow as "shared" items. My middle daughter wants a slingshot, and I'll probably share that, too. Maybe I'll get a pellet gun to share with my youngest daughter . . . and that rat that eats the tomatoes in our garden.

．　．　．

Here's my final recommendation: be careful doing the 100 Thing Challenge. It's quite possible that once you're done, you will find yourself content without much stuff. You'll find that you no longer have a compulsion to get more and more. Then you'll have to figure out something other than shopping to do with your time, money, and talents.

My Post-Challenge "Ideal" List

BASICS

Bible

Wedding ring

Journal

Pencil

Pen

TECHNOLOGY

Watch

Laptop

Mobile phone

Camera

Lens

Tripod

Headphones

TRANSPORTATION

Car

Skateboard

PERSONAL ITEMS

Sunglasses

Toothbrush

Razor

Travel/work
backpack

Garment bag

Suitcase

ADVENTURE GEAR

Backpacking
pack

Tent

Sleeping bag

Sleeping pad

Stove

Cook set

Spork

Water bladder

Headlamp

Knife

Knife

ADVENTURE CLOTHES

Fleece jacket

Rain jacket

Thermal shirt

Thermal pants

Wool hat

Mittens

Running
shorts

Running shoes

Running shoes

Hiking boots

SURFING

Board shorts

Wetsuit, full

Wetsuit jacket

Surfboard

WORK CLOTHES

Suit

Sport coat

Tie

Tie

Dress shirt

Dress shirt

Dress shirt

Dress shirt

Dress pants

Dress pants

Dress shoes
(black)

Dress belt
(black)

CASUAL CLOTHES

Casual jacket

Sweater

Sweater

Button-down
LS shirt

Button-down
LS shirt

Button-down
LS shirt

Button-down
LS shirt

Button-down
LS shirt

Button-down
SS shirt

Button-down
SS shirt

Button-down
SS shirt

Button-down
SS shirt

Button-down
SS shirt

Jeans

Jeans

Jeans

Casual pants

Casual pants

Casual belt
(brown)

Casual shoes
(brown)

Casual shoes
(brown)

Sandals

PJ pants

T-shirt

T-shirt

T-shirt

T-shirt

T-shirt

T-shirt

T-shirt

T-shirt

Undershirts

Underwear

Socks

Hat

MISCELLANEOUS

Books

Moo business
cards

Guitar

Acknowledgments

I would like to thank my friend John Watson. He was the first to be amused by my 100 Thing Challenge and instigated all the attention that has followed. This book would not have been written without his first step. I am grateful.

Once others took note of my 100 Thing Challenge, I was not sure what to do. I am indebted to Lisa Sharkey, who recognized a book before I saw one. I am thankful that she talked me into writing it and remained committed to this project, even when it was tough. I would like to thank my editors: Amy Bendell's patience and insight have made this a better story. Special thanks to Ian Jackman. I needed his eye to put everything together. And also I'm glad for Greg Daniel's wisdom.

To my friend Tim Morriss, your one sentence of encouragement did more than all else to make me brave enough to write this book. Thank you.

To all of my friends, acquaintances, and the hundreds of perfect strangers who have called and commented and e-mailed your advice, I give my hearty appreciation. We need each other.

Of course my family is entitled to thanks most of all. I am so in love with my three daughters, who remained carefree and continued to live childlike lives throughout, only occasionally pausing to glance curiously at their father's antics. My dear wife has always been faithful and supportive (though not an enabler) of my crazy ideas. She deserves my thanks. She also has my heart forever.